On a Wing

and a Prayer

Stories from Freedom Fellowship

A Prison Ministry

Becky Lyles

PERPEDIT ✓ PUBLISHING, INK

Cover design by Joel Abeyta

Perpedit Publishing, Ink

ISBN 978-0-615-52378-1
Library of Congress Catalog Card Number: 2005270938

*If the Son sets you free,
you will be free indeed. John 8:36 (NIV)*

*The Spirit of the Lord God is upon me, because the Lord has anointed
me to bring good news to the afflicted. He has sent me to bind up the
brokenhearted, to proclaim liberty to the captives, and freedom to
prisoners. Isaiah 61:1 (NASB)*

*Not by might nor by power, but by my Spirit,
says the Lord Almighty. Zechariah 4:6b (NIV)*

Some wish to live within the sound

of church or chapel bell.

I want to run a rescue shop

within a yard of hell.

C. T. Studd

The stories in this book are those of real people; however, some names have been changed.

Dedication

This book is dedicated to:

My mother, LaVerne; my sons, Bruce and Brian, my daughter-in-law, Wanda; my grandchildren, Scot and Amanda; and my brother, Bill, for unselfishly allowing me to give time that could have been spent with them to fulfill the vision God gave me to set the captives free;

The members of the Board of Directors for Freedom Fellowship—Dave, Ginny, Vanita, Helain, Bart, Debbie, Angel and Nancy—who help me make the many important decisions that are necessary to keep Freedom Fellowship running smoothly. Most of these people have been with me from the very beginning and have been truly dedicated co-laborers in this ministry;

Pastors David Huntwork, John Stocker, Mark Lucks, Bill Kline, Dary Northrop, Darren Fred and others whose advice and support I truly value;

And to all of my dear friends who have always been there to encourage and support me and Freedom Fellowship.

Chaplain Donna Roth
Founder and Director
Freedom Fellowship
Fort Collins, Colorado

Acknowledgments

Interviewing the individuals represented in these pages was a wonderful privilege for me. Through their stories, I've been inspired, challenged, encouraged in my walk with God, convicted of my lack of appreciation for his many blessings in my life, and moved deeply by the bravery my new friends display as they daily confront daunting difficulties.

I am amazed that they so willingly laid bare their souls and their histories for me to expose to their community and beyond. I am awed by their desire to tell the world the good news that Jesus can reach down into the dismal dungeons of this dark planet to bring light and life, healing, comfort, guidance, power and strength, hope and faith, encouragement, and so much more. I am also touched by the depth of their gratitude to God for the miracles he has performed in their lives.

My thanks to each of you for your honesty, your transparency, your vulnerability, and the tears you shared with me, a stranger. Thank you for letting me vicariously experience your pain and your sorrows, your triumphs and your joys. I am a better person because you recounted your life journey to me and allowed me to shape it into written form for others to read and thereby become better people, also.

A great group of proofreaders assisted me by reading through and commenting on the original manuscript. Their insights, questions and suggestions helped create a more readable, more understandable book. Thank you Anthony Johnson, Larry Baker, Linda Boraiko, Cheryl Collins, Vanita Fowden, Allen Harris, Alissa Lyles, Steve Lyles, Marianne

Murah, Ron Sammons and Debbie Watts for volunteering your time and talent to help expand the kingdom of God through the ministry of Freedom Fellowship.

Becky Lyles
Cheyenne, Wyoming

I would like to acknowledge and thank the following people, for without their input there would not only be no book, but in some cases, there would be nothing to write about:

Becky Lyles, for the hours she spent interviewing people and compiling their testimonies, and for her patience with the multiple delays in getting the final draft ready for the printer. My prayer is that God will bless her many times over for her selfless, giving spirit;

The Freedom Fellowship volunteers who give of their time and talent to make this ministry possible. The love they have for inmates and ex-inmates is evident and has helped many who feel like the off-scouring of the world to realize that God does love them and that they are redeemable;

The many financial supporters of this ministry, who faithfully give to make it possible for us to continue to go to the jails and prisons and share the love of Christ;

Those who have been benefactors of this ministry, and who have been willing to share their stories so others may know that there is no such thing as a hopeless case; and, Most of all, I wish to thank the Lord Jesus Christ for enabling me to do a ministry that has so greatly blessed my life.

Chaplain Donna Roth
Founder and Director
Freedom Fellowship
Fort Collins, Colorado

Contents

Foreword, Pastor John Stocker, Resurrection Fellowship xiii
Introduction, Chaplain Donna Roth, Founder, Director 1

Chapter 1   True Freedom
                    Chris, Ex-Inmate 7

Chapter 2   Can I Hold Your Hand?
                    Pamela, Ex-Inmate, Board of Directors 15

Chapter 3   God, You're Somethin' Else
                    John, Ex-Inmate 27

Chapter 4   Smile, Jesus Loves You
                    Shanna, Ex-Inmate 41

Chapter 5   God Chooses Nobodies
                    Angel, Board of Directors 49

Chapter 6   Life Is Good
                    Andy, Ex-Inmate 57

Chapter 7   The Mountain of Prison
                    Sarah and Mandy, Inmates 65

Chapter 8   No More "Buts"
                    Harold, Inmate 69

Chapter 9   Just Love Them
                    Debbie and Bart, Board of Directors 79

Chapter 10   Giving Back
                    Art, Ex-Inmate 87

Chapter 11   Walking in the Spirit
                    Chaplain Donna Roth, Founder, Director 95

Chapter 12   Growing Up
                    Brad, Ex-Inmate 103

Chapter 13   A Commitment to Be Real
                    Pastor Dave, Board of Directors 108

Chapter 14   His Name Was Carlos
                    Shelly, Inmate's Spouse 115

Chapter 15   That's Why I Call Him "Father"
                    David, Ex-Inmate, Former Board Member 119

Chapter 16   Road to Freedom
             Shirley, Volunteer.................................131
Chapter 17   Free on the Inside
             Joseph, Inmate....................................137
Chapter 18   You Are My Provider
             Chaplain Donna Roth, Founder, Director.......145
Chapter 19   Just Walking with God
             Vanita, Board of Directors 151
Chapter 20   Does She Have Tattoos?
             Scott, Donna Roth's Grandson 155
Chapter 21   The Most Amazing Thing
             Katherine, Ex-Inmate............................161
Chapter 22   It Doesn't Get Any Better than This
             Shawn, Ex-Inmate 169
Chapter 23   Adult Church
             Chaplain Donna Roth, Founder, Director.......179
Chapter 24   There Is No Tomorrow
             Steve, Ex-Inmate.................................183
Chapter 25   I Could Have Danced All Night
             Edith, Former Board Member......................195
Chapter 26   My Heart Is in Prison
             Mike, Ex-Inmate, Volunteer 201
Chapter 27   On the Other Side
             Christine and John, Ex-Inmates 207
Chapter 28   God Opened My Heart
             Richard, Ex-Inmate 213
Chapter 29   New Creations in Christ
             Ginny, Board of Directors 221
Chapter 30   Uganda Diary Highlights
             Chaplain Donna Roth, Founder, Director.......225
Chapter 31   It Just Keeps Getting Better
             Ron, Ex-Inmate..................................231
Chapter 32   Hooray, Colorado
             Helain, Board of Directors 237
Chapter 33   I'm Not Going to Prison
             Gary, Ex-Inmate 241

Conclusion, Chaplain Donna Roth, Founder, Director...................*253*

Foreword

Over the last 20-plus years, I have had the wonderful privilege of watching God do an amazing work through Donna that no one could have imagined. As I view her ministry in retrospect, I am convinced that her humble personality is one of her greatest assets. Because of her unpretentious nature, she is not a threat to those in authority or to the inmates to whom she has been called to minister. Without question, her calm, quiet approach has opened many doors for her. The wisdom of God never ceases to amaze me.

I believe this book will be a tremendous blessing to all who read it. The book is not about Donna; rather, it is about Jesus Christ and the wonderful way he touches lives. To the world, many people in this book appeared to be rejects to be discarded, but to God they were wonderful opportunities to show his love and glory in an unmistakable way.

If you like to see the finger of God moving in human lives, then you will enjoy this book. It is the story of a faithful, loving Father who never gives up on his children.

Pastor John Stocker
Resurrection Fellowship
Loveland, Colorado

Introduction

Lord, You Have the Wrong House
Chaplain Donna Roth, Founder and Director

I was sound asleep when the Lord called my name 23 years ago in a voice so loud it woke me up. After he got my attention, he said, "I'm going to send you to jail to tell people about me."

I said, "Lord, you have the wrong house!"

Jails frightened me. People with tattoos frightened me. I was the "square" kind of mom who made my two sons tuck in their shirts and wear their hair short. Plus, I was a brand new Christian who knew nothing about ministry.

My youngest son had just been diagnosed with severe juvenile diabetes, so I was busy learning how to care for him. I was also trying to help my older son, who was dabbling in drugs and running with the wrong crowd. On top of all that, I worked full time, and my marriage was disintegrating.

Needless to say, I didn't need any more turmoil in my life. Yet, despite the upheaval and the fact that I hadn't had any interest in a prison ministry before that night, the Lord filled my heart with love for inmates. A burning desire to minister to them in the jails and prisons grew within me.

I met with my pastor and told him what the Lord had told me, even to the point of outlining the details of the ministry, which included a promise of local, state, national and international outreach.

He smiled then said, "That's very interesting," as he handed me a letter he'd recently received from a woman who wanted to start a Prison Fellowship chapter in Fort Collins.

When I called her, she started to cry. She'd sent out 300 letters asking others to help her start a PF chapter but had not received a single response. She said, "I told the Lord this morning, 'If no one calls by tonight, I'm going to drop the whole thing.'"

The two of us, with four other volunteers, started Prison Fellowship in Fort Collins in 1980. We ministered to inmates in the Larimer County Detention Center (LCDC) as well as in state prisons throughout Colorado and Wyoming.

In 1989, God again awakened me in the night, this time to tell me to form Freedom Fellowship. He wanted a ministry where we could lead people to the Lord *and* to baptism in the Holy Spirit. I told God, "You're going to have to do something about all those prison chaplains who aren't open to a Spirit-filled ministry." It wasn't long before the State of Colorado laid off all its paid chaplains and began using volunteer chaplains who, for the most part, respect our ministry.

We recently received a letter from the Department of Corrections giving us permission to pray with the inmates for Spirit baptism. According to the letter, no one is to interfere with that aspect of our ministry. Such a directive from the state can only be the work of God.

After serving as a Freedom Fellowship volunteer for 18 years, one day as I walked down a hallway in the local jail, I heard the Lord say, "Donna, I have made you chaplain of this jail."

I said, "Lord, nobody here told me that!"

But I took a step of faith and called one of the prison chaplains to ask him what chaplains do. He was kind enough to send me literature on the subject. After reading through the information, I thought, *I do a lot of that already.* The next thing I knew, LCDC asked me to become its chaplain. The experience has been a tremendous blessing in my life.

I'm in jail all week and in prison all weekend. Oftentimes, I'm on suicide watch at the jail. A typical example of working with suicidal people is the story of one troubled but reluctant inmate the guards brought to me.

"I don't want to see no chaplain!" he insisted. "I don't want to see no religious person."

The guards said, "We just want you to spend a few minutes with Chaplain Roth."

The man stood in a corner glaring at me. "I don't want to see you. I don't even want to talk with you."

I sat calmly in my chair and spoke quietly with him, just sharing the love of Jesus. After a while, he relaxed and sat down across from me. It wasn't long before I was able to lead him to the Lord and in the baptism of the Holy Spirit. When the guard returned, the inmate asked, "Could I have another hour with Donna?"

Today, that man is leading a Bible study in prison and reading every Christian book he can get his hands on. He has a long prison sentence ahead of him, but he has the Lord, and he has a peace in his life he never had before.

My goals are to empty the jails and to keep inmates from returning to jail once they've been released. We help them find churches to attend when they get out. It's not unusual for them to become leaders in the churches. One ex-inmate is now doing street ministry. He's a real evangelist.

Others are successful pastors, businessmen and businesswomen.

More and more people are coming out of prison on fire for God. They're setting the churches on fire. They want to be busy serving the Lord and leading others to him. I see them igniting the church from the pew.

Some ex-inmates slip and go back to their old ways. They have to learn to break the ties from their former lives, to make right choices, to live by God's Word and his Spirit. Our support group encourages them to stay faithful to the Lord.

It's so rewarding to see people become what God created them to be. My heart is blessed every day. There's nothing else I would rather do. I have seen some inmates with life sentences become Christians at LCDC. When they're transferred from jail to prison, they're excited to go and to be used by God. If they're to be in prison forever, so be it. They just want God to use them for his glory.

The justice system is beginning to recognize Freedom Fellowship's value. Community corrections officials recently gave us an award for aiding the justice system. They are noticing that people are changed through our ministry.

When criminals who were previously arrogant, belligerent and smart-mouthed stand respectfully before them, saying, "I found the Lord in jail. I want to apologize for what I did and be fully responsible for my actions," the judges see their humility and sometimes hand down lighter sentences. Freedom Fellowship volunteers pray for the judges when they make their decisions. We've seen some real miracles. It's all God's doing.

In 1998, Freedom Fellowship was nominated for the Group Publishing, Inc. Outstanding Community Service award. The day the award was to be given, we had $89 in our ministry bank account. As Ginny and I drove to the awards ceremony, I said, "Maybe Freedom Fellowship will be given a little something at this luncheon."

We were shocked and blessed to be awarded $10,000. When I handed the check to our treasurer, I said, "Now you can pay the phone bill."

Freedom Fellowship has grown. We started out with six people. Today, we have around 120 volunteers. We are constantly enlisting more volunteers, more speakers and more music teams. We're also providing more seminars than ever before. We started our first national chapter in Pennsylvania a couple years ago, and we went to Africa last summer to start our first international chapter.

When the Lord called me, he told me he would bring committed volunteers. We have had the same core group from the very beginning, but we get excited every time new people join us. I love to see others join Freedom Fellowship, because they get to do what I do every day—watch God in action. It especially touches my heart when ex-inmates become volunteers. Through God's power, they find themselves doing great on the outside, and they want to go back to the prisons to share his love.

I want to emphasize that a person doesn't have to be perfect to be used in ministry. God knows your heart, he knows you want to serve him, and he'll take you right where you are. You don't have to have a flawless family for God to use you. That certainly wasn't the case with my family. In fact, when the Lord called me, he also told me, "Your husband may not be with you."

Over the years, Freedom Fellowship has had a few steady financial supporters, but we trust God for most of our income. Several former inmates contribute financially to Freedom Fellowship. Their commitment amazes me, as does God's constant provision.

The most important aspect of Freedom Fellowship is prayer. We've learned that the harder the devil attacks, the bigger the victory waiting right around the corner. So we praise the Lord when Freedom Fellowship is attacked, but we stay on our knees. If we don't pray, there will be no victory.

What I do in the jails and prisons is a privilege, not work. My heart is constantly warmed by the way God turns people's lives around to be conformed to what he has created them to be. I can never say, "I'm going to work," because I enjoy jail ministry so much and find it so fulfilling.

Following are stories from some of the many wonderful people God has placed in my life through the ministry of Freedom Fellowship. They are remarkable folks from both sides of the bars who have heard God's voice and learned to walk in his freedom and power. They are also generous individuals who graciously give you glimpses into their worlds, worlds where pain, heartache and regret have been replaced with peace, perseverance and happiness. Enjoy!

Chapter 1

True Freedom
Chris, Ex-Inmate

In 1993, I had an illicit relationship with a 17-year-old female student at the Christian high school where I taught math, science, physical education and history. I was also the athletic director and coached the boys' varsity basketball team. When the affair was discovered, I was arrested, jailed, and charged with sexual assault of a minor then released on bond for eight months.

Prior to my court sentencing, I met with an attorney who said the worst case scenario he could foresee for me was three months in jail and 90 days probation. I had a lot going for me: a college degree, no previous record, I had not committed a violent act, and there was no intercourse involved.

I had never before committed any sort of crime. In fact, I had become a Christian as a teenager and attended a Christian college in Ohio. I was head of several campus groups at that school, including the volunteer outreach program, the retreat committee, and Christian Households (similar to fraternities).

But like the prodigal son, after I graduated from college, I put God on the back burner. I never directly rebelled or ran from him or stopped believing. I just didn't make him Lord of my life. When God is not in the driver's seat, people make poor choices, which I certainly did.

In November of 1994, I walked into a courtroom filled with my family and friends. The judge said that, in all his years on the bench, he'd never received so many letters regarding a defendant. Despite such an outpouring of support, he sentenced me to eight years with the Colorado Department of Corrections. I can't begin to express in Webster's English how devastated I felt.

I understood, however, that I had violated a position of trust, and that my sin was more than just breaking a law. I had failed in my covenant with my wife and my God. I had also betrayed the trust of my children, my church, my community, the other teachers, the students, their parents—the list goes on and on. That violation of trust was one reason my punishment was so severe, even though no one expected it to be so harsh.

After the sentencing, I was taken to Larimer County Detention Center. Depressed, shocked, and shattered by the judge's decision, I cried myself to sleep my first night in jail, and many nights thereafter. The guards thought I might be suicidal, so they put me on suicide watch and asked Donna Roth to visit me.

Donna helped me make it through those first few weeks of incarceration. She's a special lady. Through her, my Abba Father talked to me and touched my heart. I felt close to God when I was with her.

Donna has the ability to "read your mail." Every time she meets with an inmate—male or female, young or old—she takes him or her Bible verses. She works all day at the jail and then goes home at night and prays for the inmates. God gives her Scriptures for each person.

I'm not talking about one or two verses. She usually has a list of 10 to 20 Scriptures. Most of the time, she doesn't look them up beforehand. God just tells her "Proverbs 6:8" or whatever, and she writes it down, usually on a little yellow Post-It Note. We used to call her the "Post-It Note Queen."

And the verses were always right on. They were encouraging, convicting, soothing, powerful—whatever was needed at that moment. They brought tears of joy and hope in a despairing place and time, and unconditional love in an unloving world.

That's the way it was for me the first time she brought me Scriptures. They were all just what I needed right then. She handed me the list and said, "Here are your Scriptures. Why don't we go through them together? Let's see what God has to say to you."

"Oh, Lord," I prayed silently, "I know you're with me, and I know you're speaking to me through this woman and your Word."

Something else interesting about Donna—guards will occasionally bring angry, volatile individuals, even murderers, to her. They remove the man's handcuffs, lock him in a room with Donna and walk away, knowing the inmate will be more peaceful after the visit.

Donna will sit there as calm as the wind after a storm and just love the guy. Even violent men are instantly broken down by the power of God's presence in that room. They know God is there. They sense his angels surrounding them, and they know not to mess with Chaplain Roth.

When guys put razors to their wrists, the guards page Donna. She goes on suicide watches almost weekly. She ministers God's love to hurting people and keeps them from taking their lives. She not only keeps them from killing themselves, but offers them a whole new way of life, eternal life.

I attended all the Freedom Fellowship Bible studies while at LCDC. I also started a Bible study group with another inmate. After eight months in the county facility, I was transferred to the state prison in Canon City.

I'd only been at Canon City for three months when another devastating thing happened. During a visit with my wife and kids, a guard walked up. "Enjoy your last hour with your family," he said. "You're going to Texas in the morning."

Much like the movie "Con Air," early the next morning several of us were shackled, marched onto a plane by a SWAT team, escorted by another team of big guys, and flown to the Bowie County Correctional Center in Texarkana, Texas. I saw my family one time in the two years I was down there.

I could write a book about the Texas penal system. We were beaten, Maced and tear-gassed. There were riots, suicides and fires caused by arson. I was stabbed by a Muslim. Guards stole our money, our books and other possessions. Cockroaches crawled out of the food. You name it, we encountered it in Texas.

We lived in cages, 24 men to a cage. Even the ceiling was made of bars. We had one toilet in the back of the room and one shower. It was a dump of a place, an old railroad warehouse right next to the train tracks that had been converted into a private jail. The State of Colorado abandoned us in a filthy facility where the guards' only training, I was told, was to watch the movie "Shawshank Redemption" and to be sprayed in the face with Mace, so they would know what it feels like and therefore hesitate to use it.

We were in that prison for nine long months. One thing about that Texas prison was good. We had Bible pods—three pods or cages of 24 men each, where we studied the Bible for four hours each day. It was great. In addition, the Lord gave me another unique opportunity to share his love.

While I was reading my Bible on my bunk one day, the chaplains walked by. My cellmates were clamoring at the bars, begging for the chaplains' assistant job. One of the chaplains looked at me (he later told me a light was shining on me) and said, "Hey, you! Come here." He asked me to go to their office to interview for the position, and I was hired.

That job enabled me to lead a lot of men to the Lord. Much like the librarian in "Shawshank Redemption," I pushed a book cart around. I also sharpened pencils for my fellow prisoners. Moving from cage to cage, from solitary cell to solitary cell, I talked with each inmate. Through those interactions, I led 55 Texas and Colorado inmates to the Lord plus a guard who came into the chaplain's office in tears one day.

After I'd been there almost nine months, the prisoners rioted and took over the facility. I was not a part of the riot nor was anyone in the Bible pods. The other inmates actually forced the guards off the floor, knocked down walls, and demolished the place. After months of abuse and torment, Mace-damaged eyes, filth, rotten food, protest and outcries, the men revolted. A lot of illegal stuff happened on both sides of the bars in that prison.

Finally, the ACLU came in. They discovered mice, cockroaches, and standing water in the kitchen, and many other sordid deficiencies. Shortly thereafter, they filed a class action lawsuit for some of the inmates stating the facility wasn't fit for dogs or rats.

The prison was soon condemned and shut down. We were transferred to the Karnes City Correctional Facility in San Antonio, Texas. I spent about 14 months in that prison working as a GED teacher. One weekend, Freedom Fellowship volunteers drove all the way from Colorado to San Antonio to do a seminar for us. They saw how atrocious and poor the conditions were at that facility, like in a third-world country.

I just did my time in Texas, tried to do my best. I read my Bible completely through three times and grew in my walk with the Lord in ways I can't explain. I would never want to go through that experience again, but it was the most growing time in my life.

I read 300 to 400 books in prison. I also wrote some poems that were published in Washington, D.C. and a gospel tract that a chaplain in Texas published. I'm now in the process of writing two books.

One is titled "Exposing the Darkness." It's about revealing the darkness within each one of us so we can experience freedom, exposing the darkness within the Body of Christ as a whole, and exposing the darkness within our country's penal system. The other one, called "The Game Plan," is about how to be victorious in the spiritual warfare game.

After three years in prison, I was returned to LCDC in Colorado for reconsideration of my case. While I waited for the hearing, Donna visited me and taught me about the Lord. Then I taught 10 to 13 guys who gathered around a table every night to study the Word of God together.

I was released in 1997 and soon found myself leading Freedom Fellowship's ex-inmate support group. At first, it was just a support group, but then several people requested we do more study in the Word. So I taught that group for two years under Donna's tutelage. It's a group for those who want to stay on the straight and narrow road and continue to seek God, to serve and follow him.

The group is a place where ex-inmates and their family members can be comfortable and transparent, where they can voice hurts, fears and frustrations. They can be vulnerable and real, be accepted right where they're at, and be loved with the love of Christ. They encourage each other and keep each other accountable.

Colorado leads the nation with 85 percent recidivism, which means rate of return to prison. Freedom Fellowship's recidivism rate is less than 4 percent for those who stay involved with the organization.

Freedom Fellowship volunteers take the unconditional love of God to the jails and the prisons. Their attitude is: *We don't care where you've been. We don't care what you've done. We just want you to know God loves you right where you're at, right in the midst of what you're going through. He knows your past. He's already nailed it on the cross.*

That's their attitude, and that's what gives them power. When you lead people by the love of God and through the nurturing of God, they always want more. They want to come closer to the throne.

The ministry is called Freedom Fellowship because God wants us to walk in freedom. As a result of what I've been through, *I know that I know that I know true freedom is spiritual freedom.*

There are guys in prison who, because of their walk with the Lord, are freer than many people on the outside. I correspond with six guys who will never walk on the streets of Planet Earth again, but someday they'll dance on the streets of gold. They understand and experience true freedom.

God spoke to me one day in Texas as I lay on a top bunk in my cage watching the guards through the bars. They were mean, nefarious men who reveled in antagonizing us, who left the lights on at night and dribbled basketballs in the hallways so we couldn't sleep. God said, "I don't see things the way you see them."

I asked, "What do you mean, Lord?"

He said, "Look at those guys. I see you as being on the outside of the bars and them on the inside. They are like Lazarus, wrapped in the grave clothes, the bondage, and the strongholds of sin that have held them for years. You are free in my eyes."

I thank God for the freedom, love and forgiveness I found in him through his Word and through the guidance of Freedom Fellowship. I continue to walk in that freedom and to share it with others who are bound by sin.

Chapter 2

Can I Hold Your Hand?
Pamela, Ex-Inmate

I grew up in a small farming community in Kansas. My parents were farmers and devout Methodists, who took me to church with them throughout my childhood. When I was 18, I married my high-school sweetheart, Warren. We had our first child, Luanne, a year later. Our son, Nathan, was born three years later, during the Vietnam War.

Shortly after Nathan's birth, Warren enlisted in the Marine Corps. When he completed boot camp, he was stationed in Beaufort, South Carolina. Luanne, Nathan and I joined him there, but Warren was soon sent to Vietnam. The children and I remained in Beaufort, where I owned and operated a daycare center. I also worked part time as a waitress.

One evening, I allowed Luanne to sleep at her friend Tanya's house. What was to be a night of six-year-old fun and giggles turned into a nightmare when Tanya's mother's boyfriend brutally raped my daughter.

Shortly after I brought Luanne home from the emergency room, the man who raped her came to our house to tell me he didn't do it. Then he offered to have sex with me to compensate for the molestation of my beautiful daughter. I became very upset, and we got into a heated argument that ended when I shot and killed him.

That sounds like a simple statement, but that's what happened. My parents cared for my children while I served five years for manslaughter.

I can't begin to say what prison was like for a 23-year-old Methodist white girl from Kansas incarcerated in the South during that dark time of war and racial tension. I didn't think I would live that first year, but in order to survive, a person changes. I changed for the worse, becoming angry and full of hate.

I couldn't understand how God could let something like that happen to me. I think that's when I began to doubt God's existence. Later on, I hated God. How I could deny that there is a God and hate him at the same time, I don't know, but I did.

I like to think I might have been a different person if my experiences in the South Carolina prison had not been so horrible. Among other atrocities, I saw two murders. In one case, I was standing next to a young inmate when her lover, over whatever anger or jealousy was going on between them, threw a pot of boiling water on her. The meat literally fell off of the girl's bones, clear down to her organs.

There was nothing safe about that prison. The guards controlled every move we made, whether it was to go to the bathroom or to eat. We were totally at their mercy. I don't remember how many times I was beaten and/or raped by guards. We were at risk every moment. I believe the person I was, or maybe could have been, died in South Carolina.

When I got out of prison, I moved back to Kansas to be near my family. Luanne and Nathan were still with my parents, because Warren had divorced me and abandoned our children when he returned from Vietnam. I began life on the outside as a single mom, working in construction with my brothers. I also started to drink.

Eventually, I married a man named Lou, who had been raised by a madam in a house of prostitution. His understanding of relationships was much different than mine, and he became abusive.

My parents had a wonderful relationship, so I'd never been exposed to marital abuse. The mistreatment increased my anger and my tendency toward violence. I hated everybody and everything. I was angry *all* the time. I don't remember a day when I was not angry.

Lou and I lived together for around 12 years. We both drank and we both used cocaine. We considered it a party drug, a weekend type of thing. It didn't seem to affect our lives too much.

Then our use began to go deeper. And I started dabbling in criminal activity. I don't think I got into crime to pay for the drugs as much as I did to act out my rebellion and anger. My subconscious attitude was, *I'm going to take what I want and pay back the establishment for everything it's done to me.*

I shoplifted as a business, selling my products to people in the church, to attorneys, to judges, to bondsmen. They knew the source, and it was okay with them. They were getting a bargain. That's not to say I wasn't responsible for my own actions, but it made it easier for me to feel like I was doing the right thing when I sold merchandise to those kinds of people.

I saw white collar crimes happening all around me and people going free for atrocities I never even considered doing. So I rationalized that it was all right for me to do what I was doing. I thought the way I "earned" money was actually benefiting people. I was Robin Hood. It was a warped philosophy and a means of denying my addiction. *I don't really need cocaine. I just do drugs because I have the extra cash.*

Throughout our marriage, Lou kept women who worked as prostitutes for him. I saw a lot of different levels of prostitution. I will never forget running into a judge in the home of one of Lou's prostitutes. I had previously stood before that official in court. A United States senator was also a client. I'd see those things and I'd think, *I'm on the right track. This is the way life is supposed to be.*

Our marriage deteriorated, and my criminal activities escalated. I began to have more legal problems, occasionally spending time in jail for shoplifting, driving under the influence, and other minor charges.

I moved to Denver in 1990. Shortly thereafter, Lou followed. Our drugging and drinking intensified to extreme levels. In 1993, doctors discovered I had colon cancer. Lou left me and moved in with a 16-year-old girl whose child he'd fathered.

My own children were grown and gone by then, so I had surgery and went through chemotherapy and radiation all alone. The cancer was destroyed, but I didn't care whether I was cured or not.

When I recovered, I got involved with a man named Arnold. He was a gang member and dealt drugs on a large scale. I don't know how I lived through the next two years. I maintained a $600-per-day cocaine habit and can't remember a day when I didn't drink. The crime spree was unbelievable. We did everything from theft and forgeries to fraud, prostitution and drug deals. The only thing I didn't do was rob a bank, thank God.

Our relationship was horrible. One time Arnold beat me with a baseball bat. He crushed one side of my face and broke six ribs, my leg and my arm. I was in the hospital for two-and-a-half months, but I didn't mind. I used the pain as a reason to continue the drugs.

I knew Arnold was dangerous. He was so arrogant. Yet I went back to him after I got out of the hospital. I wanted him to kill me. I didn't care. I was so tired.

One night he sent me outside to get some coke he'd left in the car. When I walked back in, he jumped from behind the door, grabbed me, and crammed a gun into my mouth. "Who were you with out there?" he screamed. "Who did you sell the drugs to? Where are they?" He pulled the trigger, but the gun jammed. Drugs do crazy things to a person's mind.

We moved to Compton, a Los Angeles suburb, for six months. Compton is a war zone, another world. Whatever kept me from being killed or killing someone, I don't know. I always carried a gun and a knife, and I kept a shotgun in my car.

One day a drug deal went bad in Compton. I can't remember if the other guys thought Arnold was ripping them off, or if they were trying to rip us off. We were standing there doing a money and drug exchange, and they started shooting. We shot back. Two people died in that incident. I wasn't even grazed by a bullet, though we were standing less than a yard from the others.

Then Arnold went to prison for an attempted murder charge. I knew there were also warrants out for my arrest, so I went into hiding in Wyoming. But I got involved in a drug deal there and was arrested on a drug charge, which carried 20 years.

That was the least of my problems. I had nine felony warrants in three other states. And the FBI wanted me for continued criminal activity (racketeering).

I was in big, big trouble. My parents posted bond and hired an attorney for me. I returned to Colorado to await trial. During that time, I had a shoplifting charge in Fort Collins. My attorney assured me that it wasn't a problem. I would just pay a fine and go on about the business of taking care of the more serious charges that were going to put me in prison.

I went to court drunk and high. The judge took one look at me and was not happy. He said, "If I could, I would gladly put you in prison for the rest of your life." Instead, he gave me a 30-day sentence at the Larimer County Detention Center in Fort Collins.

When I was taken to LCDC, I was still facing the drug charge in Wyoming plus other charges in Nebraska and Colorado. I was depressed, and I didn't want to talk with anyone. The gal who did the intake at LCDC informed me she was going to ask Chaplain Roth to visit with me, or she was going to put me on a suicide watch. I bluntly told her what she could do with both ideas.

Thirty minutes later, I was told I had a visitor. A guard escorted me into a room furnished with a small table and two chairs and introduced me to Donna Roth. I told her, in not-so-polite terminology, "You're wasting your time. I didn't ask for you to be here. I would like you to leave."

Donna reached across the table. "Can I hold your hand for a moment?"

At the instant she touched my hand, I felt incredible warmth, like somebody was pouring love and heat through me. She asked me, "Can we say the sinner's prayer together?"

"I don't know what that is."

"Just repeat it after me."

While Donna was talking, in my mind I could see a door open. On my side of the door was the hell I'd lived in for so long. On the other side was a beautiful light.

It was as if God was saying, "You can choose to walk through this door, Pamela, or you can choose to stay on that side. But if you choose to stay where you're at, the door will be forever shut to you."

I chose to walk through the door, toward the light, and we prayed the sinner's prayer together. When we finished, I was in tears, though I hadn't cried in 20 years. An unbelievable peace flowed over me. I knew I had made the right choice.

I've been blessed by God because I have not used drugs since that day. I'm not saying my life turned instantly into an incredible, unending miracle, or that all my problems went away. But for the first time since I was a teenager, God was with me, and I knew it.

Everything was so different. It didn't matter if I spent the rest of my life in prison. I knew God was there, and I knew I'd been saved from the miserable life I'd been living.

Before I went back to court, the authorities did what is called a "pre-sentencing investigation." The woman who conducted my PSI wrote that she felt I was a career criminal without remorse, a sociopathic criminal with no redeemable qualities. She recommended a full sentence to the judge. If it was a life sentence, all the better. She didn't see any opportunity for rehabilitation in my case.

She was right. I was one of the most violent, dangerous people you could have in your community. I hated everybody. Nobody was going to get next to me. Nobody was going to have a chance to rape me, to hurt me, to beat me. I was going to take from them first. And I was never going to stop drinking and drugging. That was what I wanted to do, what I chose to do.

Without God, there was no hope for me. Rehabilitation would have never happened outside of his awesome power and presence. I was truly "born again." The person who lived that horrible life for 20 years is gone, a fact that still overwhelms and amazes me.

I'm not saying I'm perfect or that I don't have days when I revert back to negative thinking or unchristian attitudes. It's a daily exercise to maintain a Christ-like environment in my life. But I don't carry a gun any more, and I'm not committing crimes these days.

I ended up serving one year of a 20-year-to-life sentence. That was a miracle. I served one year in prison and one year on parole, though my attorneys had told me there was nothing they could do for me.

While I was under cover in Wyoming, I became close to a Christian man in Laramie named Jim. I called him from jail after I was arrested. He said, "Are there a few things you forgot to tell me about yourself?"

"Well, maybe one or two."

"Like your real name?"

"Well, yeah, that too."

Yet, Jim continued to encourage and help me. He was a wonderful Christian man, a retired Navy officer. He later moved to Fort Collins and became involved with Freedom Fellowship.

I opted to stay an extra four months in prison so I could parole to Fort Collins. My parole originally called for my release to Arapaho County in Denver, where I knew I would not last 10 days. I needed a Christian support system. Without it, I didn't have a chance.

I was paroled to Fort Collins in November of 1995. Within a few weeks, Jim and I became husband and wife. We attended Freedom Fellowship support group meetings and church together. We also joined an ex-felons weekly Bible study group, and I went through battered women's therapy.

In January, we learned Jim had pancreatic cancer. That was rough. I was grateful for my prison time, which had given me freedom from daily living to establish a close relationship with God through Bible study and prayer. I can't tell you how much the prison Bible studies mean to inmates. They often provide the only hope a prisoner is ever offered.

Jim was with me for 10 more months. He ministered to me and helped me understand death as a time for celebration. He helped me to be able to let go. What an awesome person he was. Jim's death was a gift to me from God, because it gave me an opportunity to learn that death is a uniting with Christ.

About three months after Jim passed away, my two-year-old grandson, Michael, was killed in a car accident because his father, Dale, was driving drunk. I got through that, but I don't think I could have done so without the lessons I learned from Jim and the time we spent talking about death and God's plan for our lives.

In my heart, I knew God took Michael home for a reason. I didn't like it, but I didn't turn into that unforgiving, angry, I-hate-the-world person again, although I came darn close. My initial, gut impulse was to get a shotgun and go shoot Dale. I thought, *God will forgive me if I kill Dale.* The first time I went to prison I didn't know about God's forgiveness, but now I did.

A few weeks later, Dale was arrested not too far from my home. When my coworkers found out he was carrying a gun, they said, "You need a gun to protect yourself. We'll loan you one."

It was tempting. I struggled with the thought of a gun, and I prayed and prayed. One night, as I was cleaning a building I cleaned every evening, I opened a closet I'd never opened before. Why I opened that closet, I will never know, but I opened it, and there stood four high-powered rifles.

I couldn't shut that door fast enough. It was like fire to me. I sucked in my breath, ran out of the building, and called my boss. "I'm going home," I told him. "I need to go home now."

I prayed all night, asking over and over, "God, what is this? What's happening here?"

Finally, it was like I could hear God saying to me, "Stop, Pamela. Just stop. Give it to me."

And I did. I said, "I can't forgive Dale right now. I can't get past the hurt. Would you take care of it, Lord?" And he did.

Dale is now serving a prison term for Michael's death. There are days when I feel I should be more forgiving toward him, and there are days when I don't care. I thank God I made it through that crisis and my family got through it. We heal a little more every day.

One of the Bible passages Donna gave me when we first met was from Hosea, where it says God will restore you and will restore your family to you. Both of my children have been to prison. Luanne, who was at one time addicted to cocaine, is free now, and we're close. Nathan is still in prison, but I know God is working in his life. Being in prison is better for him than being a junkie on the streets. At least I know he's alive.

When I was in the Arapaho County jail, our lunch was always a peanut-butter sandwich and a stale bag of chips in a paper bag we were supposed to throw away. I kept one of the bags and wrote on it the "Let Go, Let God" poem.

We set the bag on a little counter by the toilet in our cell. Women would come in, write out their problems on scraps of paper, and put them in the bag. When we had prayer time, we would pray, "Please, God, have a heart for the problems in the 'Let Go, Let God' bag."

At least twice a week, a team of officers would come into our cells unannounced and throw everything on the floor. They would flip open all the books, go through all our papers, throw mattresses off the beds, and strip our rooms. If they found any contraband, they would do strip searches on all the inmates.

The entire five months I was at Arapaho, the "Let Go, Let God" bag sat by the toilet. The guards never touched it, not one time—like it wasn't there. That was such an awesome miracle.

I have the "Let Go, Let God" poem and "Footprints" both printed on a bookmark that I carry with me all the time. Those two facets of my faith are important to me—knowing that God carried me all those years I hated him, and believing God can do anything.

When Donna prays with prisoners, she writes down Scripture passages for them on the backs of Freedom Fellowship business cards. It's so neat to get those verses. I still have all of them, and I carry them in my billfold. They're also highlighted in my Bible. I refer to them constantly.

Sometimes I get resentful and think, *What would I have become if I had gone to college, if there hadn't been a war, and I hadn't moved to South Carolina. Why couldn't my life have been different?* Down deep inside, however, I know I wouldn't trade all the horrible things from my past, because I wouldn't be where I am today, and I wouldn't do what I do today.

After everything I've been through, I have no idea why I'm alive except to serve God. That's my deepest desire. I try to serve him through Freedom Fellowship. Prison ministry is my passion, because I know how it changed my life.

Each time God takes my past, turns it around, and uses it so someone else doesn't have to experience what I did, I'm thrilled. It's an awesome privilege to be a catalyst for that miracle. For me, it's worth all the pain and heartache when—after seeing how the love of God changed my life—some of the girls in prison let his love change their lives, too.

Chapter 3

God, You're Somethin' Else
John, Ex-Inmate

M y parents moved from Texas to Colorado shortly before I was born. I had six sisters and seven brothers, and we all worked in the fields with my parents. I grew up in a really rough environment, yet I idolized my older brothers and the wild crowd they hung around with. They were always involved in shootings and stabbings. Drinking was a big thing with them. If you didn't drink, you weren't a man.

I witnessed a lot of crazy stuff. I remember guys coming over to our house and calling my brothers outside. Then the shooting would start. Afterwards, my brothers and my cousins would go over to the other guys' houses and shoot at them. It was an insane way to grow up.

I was pretty young when I started hanging around with my brothers' group. I remember ducking down onto the seat of a car I was riding in to escape the crossfire of a mobile gun battle. Berthoud, Colorado, wasn't as peaceful as you might imagine in the '60s and '70s.

I hated alcohol when I was younger, because my dad became abusive when he drank. He was a quiet, peaceful man, but when he went to bars, he ended up in trouble like my brothers. Although I hated what alcohol did to my dad, I started drinking about the time I turned 14. It was the way to be accepted in our little clique.

As soon as my mom stopped making me go to church, I quit. I didn't like church. It was just a ritual to me. Stand up, kneel down, stand up, say a prayer—same thing every week.

Besides, I was afraid of God. I thought he used lightning bolts to straighten people out. One of my older brothers told me nobody had ever read the Bible all the way through, because they would die if they did. That scared me.

From about age 15 on, I started seeing the inside of jail houses. When I was 17, I shot a guy and was charged with carrying a concealed weapon plus first-degree assault with intent to kill. The doctors didn't know if the fellow was going to live or not, so I was looking at a possible life sentence.

That was the first time I made a deal with God to get out of jail. I thought he was a make-a-deal god, a Bob Barker in the sky. "Get me out of this one, God," I prayed. "I promise I won't shoot anyone again."

After 10 days in intensive care, the guy I shot began to recover. I ended up with only six months in jail and some probation, thanks to a really good lawyer, who said it was self-defense, because the shooting happened during a brawl.

Instead of keeping my end of my bargain with God, I started acting worse. Like my dad, I became violent when I drank. I got into a lot of fights and was arrested twice for assaulting police officers. One time, I was arrested for beating a guy almost to death.

Jails were harsh back then. The guards only checked the cells every hour or two. A lot could happen during that time. Oftentimes, there were huge fights, and people would have to be carried out. It was rough. Today's jails are like daycare centers in comparison.

As tough as I was, sometimes I cried, and sometimes I prayed, not just because of loneliness, but because of all the pain I'd seen in my life. Making deals with God became a habit, but I would leave him at the jail when I got out.

One day, my oldest brother said to me, "John Boy, when you get to prison, you get yourself a job in the laundry. You can make more money that way."

I said, "I'm not going to prison."

He said, "Shut up and listen to me. The way you are, you're going to end up in prison."

Soon I discovered that snorting cocaine combined with drinking alcohol made me a mellow person. I could socialize with people without getting into fights. I started selling cocaine and went on a two-year binge of drinking and doing cocaine, along with selling it.

Eventually, I was arrested for dealing drugs. Because I drank and did cocaine 24-seven and often went 11 or 12 days without sleeping or eating, I was severely underweight when they checked me into Larimer County Detention Center.

I was also exhausted, so very tired, even though I was only 33-years old. I was finally at the point where I thought, *Money and drugs. Is this all there is to life? Is that what people are killing each other over?*

It wasn't fun anymore. It wasn't exciting any more. Living on the streets makes a person numb. You don't feel anything after a while.

I think I could have beaten the charges, because the narcotics agents had never actually seen me sell drugs. Dealers who sold for me had told them I was their supplier. But I was tired of the streets and had had enough of that lifestyle.

The public defender informed me that I had six charges, each one carrying eight to 16 years, totaling 46 to 92 years behind bars. I told the lawyer, "We can beat these charges. They don't have nothin' on me."

She came back about a month later. "They're offering you 12 years."

"Twelve years!" I said, "Forget that. I'll just sit here." So I sat in the county jail for four more months, because I couldn't post bond.

Two women who were arrested with me were also incarcerated at LCDC. The only place I could talk to them was in church. So I went to religious services and Bible studies to find out what was happening with their cases.

After attending several services, I started thinking, *These volunteers don't have to be here, but they take the time to come in to share their lives with us. There's either something to Christianity, or they're crazier than I am.*

One day a man named Ed spoke at a Freedom Fellowship meeting. He talked about putting on the armor of God. For some reason, that caught my attention, and I started listening. Like me, Ed had had a drinking problem, but God had changed him and taken over his life. Ed made a big impression on me.

In time, I didn't go to church to talk to the women. I didn't even want to talk to them. I wanted to listen to what the volunteers had to say. I went to every Bible study and religious service that was offered, and I loved it.

When friends who knew me from the streets ended up in jail, they said, "This can't be John. He's just faking it. He's trying to get a lighter sentence." But it wasn't that at all.

One day an old man who was a volunteer asked me if I had a personal relationship with Jesus.

I said, "No."

"Do you want me to pray with you?"

"Yes."

So we prayed together, and I asked Jesus to take away my sins and come into my heart. The man told me he was going to return the next week to visit me.

I said, "Yeah, right. My girlfriend doesn't even come to see me."

Sure enough, he came back. I never learned his name, but I thought, *There has to be something to this.* Then I began to feel emotions for other people and to be concerned about those around me. Before, no one else mattered to me. It was all about me, just me.

I remember Ed asking me if I knew how to pray. I told him, "No, I don't know how to pray. I don't even know what to pray. Every time I pray, I ask for something for me."

He said, "Talk to God like you would talk to your dad or to your mom. Just let him know how you feel." I tried that approach, and it was really awesome. I knew God heard my prayers, whether I prayed for other people or for myself.

I found a book in the LCDC library called "The Cross and the Switchblade" by David Wilkerson. It told the story of Nicky Cruz, a notorious gang leader in New York City. As I read about Nicky, I thought, *Wow, this guy has done as much bad stuff as I have, if not more, and God forgave him. It sounds like he's happy now.* I used the address at the back of the book to write to Nicky, but I never heard anything from him.

Finally, I was offered a six-year "open" prison sentence, which I didn't think was too bad. I knew I needed some time to straighten up. However, the lawyer told me, "With your background and all the felonies you have, the district attorney plans on aggravating that six and giving you the 12 they offered the first time."

I said "No, I can't do that."

"What will you take?"

I said, "I'll take five years, if they put a cap on it." So they handed me the five years with a cap. That meant they couldn't mess around with my sentence.

By the time I got to prison, I was into reading Scripture every day. About all I did with my time was study my Bible. I loved it. I also found another Nicky Cruz book in the prison library and discovered that the headquarters for his ministry was in Colorado Springs. So I wrote to him there.

He wrote me back and told me, "Read the book of John over and over and over again. God does love you, and he has forgiven you." He also sent me some Scripture verses. It was pretty neat to hear from Nicky.

I met some powerful, powerful Christian men in prison, guys who were so blessed and so into the Word. I'd say to them, "I want what you've got." They told me it takes reading and studying Scripture and a lot of fasting and praying and asking for God's guidance.

I've seen men doing a life stretch who are happy. They're free on the inside, like the Bible says. On the outside, they might be doing life in prison, but on the inside they're happy. They have that joy only God can give. It took prison for them to find the Lord, but they know for a fact that in the next life they'll be in heaven, not behind bars.

The whole time I was in prison, I kept praying about the anger I had built up inside of me and could not release—anger at the people who ratted me off. Even though I knew it was wrong, I swore that when I got out, I was going to kill them.

In the back of "Born Free" Bibles, there's a testimony by one of Nicky Cruz's friends, Chavez. Chavez had a friend in California who ratted on him for $250, just enough to buy an e-ball of speed.

Chavez told how he had to learn to forgive that friend. I read his story and prayed to God. "I know I'm not ready to leave here," I said. "Help me forgive these people. If I walk out of here feeling this way, I know I'll be coming back for a long, long time."

That night they called a special church event. Although I was upset and frustrated about my forgiveness problem and didn't want to go, I grabbed my Bible and walked over to the chapel. There was a guy up front giving his testimony. He looked familiar, but I couldn't place him.

Afterward, he asked if anyone needed prayer. I told him I did and explained I was having a hard time forgiving the friends who turned me in.

He told me he knew what I was talking about. "To forgive doesn't mean to forget," he said. "Human beings will never forget what people do to them. God asks you to forgive. You have to let go. To forgive is to promise you won't beat them with it anymore." We prayed together, and it felt like the anger lifted off my heart.

When I got back to my cell and opened my Bible, I saw Chavez's story and picture at the back and thought, *Whoa, this is the same guy. He came all the way from California to our little prison just when I needed him.*

"God," I exclaimed, "you're somethin' else!"

I wrote the people who ratted me off and told them I forgave them. To this day, I remember what they did to me, but I've never gone to them and said, "Hey, it's your fault I went to prison." I just let it go, and it's been such a relief.

There were many people from Mexico in the prison I was in, but only one Spanish Bible in that whole facility. Guys would come to my cell and say, "John, you seem to know quite a bit about God. Teach us about the Bible."

A Spanish fellow named Gilbert came into the prison on Wednesday nights. I said to him, "Gilbert, can you get me some Spanish Bibles?"

He said, "Yeah, I can get you Bibles."

"That would be great," I said. "These guys are really hungry for the Word in here. They also want a Bible study. Can you help us get a Bible study started?"

He said, "I'll be glad to help you."

Later that week I was sent back to Larimer County for a reconsideration. That's where the judge looks at your case and considers reducing your sentence or changing it. I spent 45 days at LCDC waiting for a court date.

One night while I was there, I was on my knees beside my bunk praying. All of a sudden, I started thanking God. I didn't ask him for anything. I just thanked him for everything he'd done for me.

Then the Spirit came over me. I felt this overwhelming joy and began to cry. I couldn't stop. The tears were flowing. I couldn't believe how much I was crying. My shirt was soaked with my tears, and I was laughing a happy, happy cry. Anybody who heard me must have thought I was crazy, being in jail and being that happy.

The guards could have opened the jailhouse doors that night and told me to go home, but I wouldn't have gone. That's how good it felt. It felt better than any drug I'd ever done. It felt better than any woman I'd ever been with, any excitement or high I'd ever experienced in my life. To this day, I believe that flood of joy was God giving me a little taste of what it will be like to be in his presence in heaven. After that experience, I understand why some people who have been resuscitated after death say they didn't want to return to life on earth.

When I finally got to court, the judge said, "Looking at your background, I think the five-year sentence fits you just right. Go on back to prison."

The week I returned, Gilbert showed up with the Spanish Bibles, and we started the Spanish Bible study. It went pretty good that first night, but I never made it to the second meeting. By the next week, I was in the Halfway House in Fort Collins. I believe the reason I went back to prison for a few days was to help the Spanish Bible study get off the ground.

After I was released, I kept reading and studying my Bible. I really had a heart for helping other people who had the same addiction I had, as well as other problems. When I discovered my employer would pay for schooling, I took classes for drug and alcohol counseling and became a counselor.

My life was going good, but I was so lonely, I would cry at night. "Lord," I'd pray, "your Word tells us that when you made Adam, you made Eve for a companion. Why am I alone?"

He knew I wasn't ready for a relationship with a woman, but I thought I was. I got into a wrong relationship and ended up backsliding all the way back to where I'd come from.

Without God's blessing and God's guidance, the relationship dragged me down, way down. One of my sisters told me, "John, you went in to save that woman, and you both ended up drowning."

I was put in the same cell at LCDC where the Spirit had flooded me with joy seven years before. It was a rude awakening to realize the wrong I'd done by not following God's guidance. I said, "God, I know I'll never again be able to feel the feeling I felt before in this cell. But please forgive me for turning my back on you."

Then I added, "God, I don't care if I spend the rest of my life alone. I don't ever want to be without you again. I just can't be without you, Lord."

That night I had a dream I'd gone to a foreign land and been dropped off a ship. All of a sudden, the enemy was after me. They were going to kill me. I ran to the ship, but just as I was getting to it, the motor started and it took off. There was no other way off the island.

Then the ship stopped, shut the motor off and let me on. For me, it was a message from God saying, "This is your last chance, John. One more time, and you won't be able to come back." I took that message to heart and have been living for the Lord the best I know how ever since.

I have a son named Johnny who was born when I was 21-years old. His mom and I didn't stay together very long, thanks to alcohol and drugs. But Johnny and I have always been really close.

When he was three months old, Johnny had open heart surgery. This was back in '78 or '79, when they didn't know a whole lot about heart surgery for infants. Before he went into the operating room, I made another one of my deals with God. *Please help my son, and I'll be a good person.* Johnny came through the surgery just fine, even though God knew I wouldn't keep my end of the bargain.

The years when I was partying were those when my son needed me the most. All I did was give him money and buy him things. I was dealing drugs and had plenty of money. I'd give him cash to go to the pool hall, or buy him rockets and robots and other stuff. I tried to buy his love.

When Johnny turned 18, he started hanging around with a hard-core group. One guy was a gang leader from California. My son told me his friend was going to California to his cousin's wedding, and he was going with him.

I thought, *Don't lie to me, son.* But I said, "I really don't want you to go, Johnny."

Johnny said, "I already told him I would go."

I said, "Johnny, I really don't want you to, but I'm here if you need me."

His mom called a couple weeks later, crying. "I'm so worried about Johnny," she said. "He hasn't called or made any contact."

As she talked and cried, I prayed. The story of the prodigal son came to my mind, the one about the kid who took off and blew his inheritance. I asked her if she had a Bible around her house. She said, "Yes."

I said, "Read Luke 15:11 through 32, and pray about it. That's all we can do."

The whole time Johnny was gone, I kept praying, "Lord, break his heart—break it wide open, but bring him back to me safe."

A friend of his called a day later. He said, "Johnny wouldn't want me to call you, but I'm worried about him. He's with the wrong people. They're sleeping in cars, because they don't have anywhere to stay."

I said, "You tell him to call me. I don't care what has happened. I just want him to call me."

Johnny called two days later, crying. He said he was sorry, and that he wanted to come home. I sent him money for a bus ticket.

The day he returned, he gave me the biggest hug and started crying. So did I. "Dad," he said between sobs, "I wish I'd listened to you."

I said, "I'm glad you didn't listen to me, Johnny. You saw what it's like on the streets, how I lived for years and years. I slept in cars every night from the time I was 14 or 15 years old. I saw gory things on the street, shooting after shooting, and other things I don't even like to talk about. It was rough, really rough. I have the battle scars to prove it."

Johnny knew about the wounds all over my body.

"It doesn't get better," I told him. "It gets worse. They may glamorize it on television, but it makes a person hard. I had the hardest heart, and God had to break it."

I thank God for breaking Johnny's heart at age 18, because it turned him around. That's when he returned to school. Johnny is 24 now and just graduated from college. He comes to see me every weekend. He loves to read Scripture with me and talk about the Bible. I feel very blessed.

I remember once asking God, "Lord, how much do you love me? How much?" He showed me pictures in my mind of those I love—my son, my family, my dad and my mom. He showed me how I am now living a peaceful life and able to sleep at night.

He also showed me how much he loves me and my brothers and sisters. In my family, instead of looking toward a high school diploma, we looked toward a prison number. All of the five older boys had run-ins with the law. I thank God my younger brothers and my sisters learned from our messed-up lives and avoided prison.

Today, everyone in my family is a strong Christian. Of my four older brothers, one is a police officer, one is the president of a bank, another is an architect, and another has worked for King Soopers for 20 years.

I've watched God work in their lives and in the lives of their wives and children. The difference God makes is just awesome. I think it was my mom's prayers that turned everything around for my family.

Without prayer and Freedom Fellowship, I would not have given my life to the Lord and experienced his love and a peaceful life. I can't say I found him, because I was the one who was lost. I never would have found my way to him. He's always been there, but he's not the God I thought he was, not the kind you can make a deal with, not the kind who zaps you with lightning.

Though the road I've walked through life has been difficult at times, I thank God it led me to him. He gave me life. There's no real life without the Lord.

Chapter 4

Smile, Jesus Loves You
Shanna, Ex-Inmate

I was raised in an abusive household, where my parents did bad, bad things to me and my siblings. I have a scar on my chin from the unopened pop can my mom threw at me when I was 15. I remember her chasing us with butcher knives. And I can still hear her screaming, "Quit complaining and eat your breakfast!" as I watched roaches fall out of the cereal box and into my bowl along with the cereal.

Ours was a pagan home. "God" and "Jesus" were just swear words, because my parents worshipped Mother Earth. They took me and my siblings to renaissance fairs—not that the fairs are necessarily bad, but mystics go to them and practice cultic activities there.

I was eight years old the first time I smoked pot. At around 12 years of age, I started using LSD and other hallucinogens. By the time I was a teenager, I was addicted to methamphetamines, or "speed" in street language.

I used speed just about any way you can think of except for slamming it. I smoked it, ate it, and snorted it. Because I didn't shoot it, I was convinced I wasn't a junkie, but that's what I was.

The first time I ran away, I was 14-years old. The authorities found me and took me home. Every time I ran away and was caught, the cops took me back. They didn't know any better. They didn't know about our home life.

Finally, I got old enough and far enough away from home they didn't bother me anymore. I roamed the country following The Grateful Dead and going to Rainbow gatherings with a guy named Shannon. We traveled together for seven years.

One dark, cold night when I was 19, we were wandering around San Francisco's Golden Gate Park looking for the bedrolls and backpacks we'd stashed behind a bush. Chilled through and through, we were anxious to return to the warm bonfire we'd been enjoying with a group of friends in the middle of the park.

Golden Gate Park is a deep park, miles long. We had to get to the front of the park in order to find our belongings. After searching for some time, we stopped to ask a woman with long, black dreadlocks for directions. Her back was to us, and she was fiddling with a bicycle.

When she turned around, her face was ugly and distorted. There was an evil aura about her that gave us a really yucky feeling. We were on a lot of hallucinogens—a whole lot—and that could have affected our perception. But we got lost using her directions. Plus, a black cat followed us, weaving in and out of the bushes beside us as we struggled to find our way.

Shannon said she was a witch, and she was going to slash our faces to "yearn off" our young beauty. That really scared me. Finally, we found our things and returned to the bonfire.

I was still feeling terribly frightened, so Shannon pulled a tract out of his pocket with the title "Smile, Jesus Loves You" on the front. We'd been panhandling on "The Haight" earlier in the day, and someone had given him a dollar and a tract.

Shannon, who'd grown up in church, told me the story of Jesus. That was the first time I can remember hearing about Christ. I didn't know anything about God. Shannon opened this tract, and we read the five or six Scriptures in it over and over again, all night long. I prayed that night to receive Christ into my heart.

I remember thinking to myself, *I want to be just like Christ, just like someone who would die for me.* I was amazed he could love me when my own parents didn't love me. Actually, I don't think it's that they didn't love me—they just didn't know how to be parents.

I sensed immediately that having Jesus in my heart was what I'd been searching for. I knew it was the truth. I never questioned it. I just believed it. And I wanted to know more. I wanted to know everything there was to know about this person who died for me.

But I continued to live the same way on the streets, stealing and doing lots of awful things to get money. I even stole a Bible out of a motel room. We eventually ended up at a Rainbow gathering in the Sangre de Cristo Mountains in Colorado, which is kind of ironic when you think about it—the "Blood of Christ" Mountains.

From there, we went to Boulder, Colorado. The weather was turning cold, so we rented a room for the winter, near the Colorado University campus. We lived with some other people and continued to commit crimes.

In early November, we wrote a bunch of bad checks in Fort Collins and stole a lot of stuff from stores then returned to Boulder. An employee at one of the stores wrote down the license number of our driver's car. When the cops located our driver, he gave them our address.

Now this is the strangest thing: In mid-November, November 17, 1994, to be exact, I was walking to 7-Eleven without shoes, because I rarely wore shoes. A woman working in her yard stopped me as I passed her house and asked if I was cold. She told me she felt like she needed to pray with me. I have no idea what made her say that to me. It had to be God, because I looked just like everybody else in that neighborhood.

When she invited me into her home, I went inside, and we knelt down together to pray. She said, "You have to give God everything."

I started crying. I told her my story, and how I was tired of the way I was living. I was a thief, a liar, a cheat, and a strung-out, skin-and-bones drug addict. I was tired of stealing money to get more drugs to make more money to get more drugs to make more money to get more drugs.

I was tired of living on the streets and happy to be living in a room for a while. But I knew we wouldn't be there for long, because we didn't have jobs or other income. She told me to talk to God every day, like I would talk to a best friend. That was the day I surrendered my life to Christ.

Later on that day, the cops came to our door. They searched our place and found all kinds of stolen stuff, but they didn't have a warrant to arrest us. Before they left, they told us they'd be back the next day to take us into custody. That's really what they said. "Be here at one o'clock tomorrow afternoon, because we are going to come back with a warrant to arrest you."

We bought some drugs, got high, and caught a bus to a KOA campground in Colorado Springs. Then we did a couple really dumb things. We lit some firecrackers, which caught the attention of the KOA manager, and we ordered a pizza with a suspicious check, which caught the attention of the restaurant manager, who called the police.

We were arrested that night. The date was November 18, 1994. That day was also my "clean day." I never used drugs again, praise God!

I spent three months in the El Paso County jail in Colorado Springs and six months in the Larimer County Detention Center, where I continued to surrender my life to God. I also began to saturate my brain with his Word. That's where I met a Freedom Fellowship volunteer named Shirley. She visited LCDC twice a week to talk with me one-on-one.

I didn't know anyone else in Fort Collins except for my co-defendant, Shannon, with whom I was not allowed to associate. Shirley made me a part of her family. She's in her 70s now and is still one of my very closest friends.

I was expected to go to prison for 25 to 32 years because I was charged with 24 felonies and the "habitual, three strikes you're out." My pre-sentencing investigation report said I was too far gone for intensive supervised probation. But an ISP officer decided to take me on her case load, despite that report.

I couldn't go to the Halfway House because Shannon was already there, so they gave me an ankle monitor. Before going back into the community, however, I was sent to a rehabilitation program, even though I knew God had delivered me from drugs. I no longer had a desire to use them.

When I returned to Fort Collins after rehab, my ISP officer picked me up at the Greyhound station and took me to a hotel. The next day, I started looking for an apartment. The first place I looked at was owned by a Christian couple. I knew for sure I wasn't going to get that place. The ad was so strict sounding, with words like "credit check" that I knew were not good words for me.

I decided I needed to be honest and tell the owner everything. He said he'd call me that night to let me know. I looked at several other apartments that same day, because I was sure I wasn't going to get the first one. But that evening, the landlord called and said he and his wife had prayed—the apartment was mine.

My first gift for the apartment was a poster that Shirley's son and daughter-in-law gave me. It had a picture of a little girl on roller skates with the caption "I got up again because of Jesus." I saw that poster first thing every morning and was reminded that I need Jesus every day.

I found a job at Wendy's right away and started going to Timberline Church with Shirley. Then I met Scott, who'd rented the apartment next to mine a month before I moved in. He was a field study biologist and gone a lot, which was probably good, because it kept our friendship from moving too fast. He started going to church with me and soon developed a personal relationship with Christ. We were married April 18, 1998.

Shirley mentored me until I got married, spending five to seven nights a week with me for the first few years. She believed I was going to make it, and she believed God wanted her to support me every way she could. Amazing. We still call each other and get together whenever we can.

46

After working at Wendy's for a year and a half, God blessed me with a job selling software. It was a much better job, paid quite a bit more, and I found there was something I could do in life beside serve hamburgers. God gave me my worth through that experience, showed me I can do anything through him.

I had to dress nice, talk with people, and go to trade shows. Suddenly, I had a career, and I was doing things I'd never imagined myself doing. It was a great experience. When we found out I was pregnant with Abigail, however, there was no doubt in our minds that God wanted me to stay home with our baby.

I'm "off paper" now, no longer on probation or ISP. I have a record, but if God wants to take care of that, he can. I've never felt like it kept me from getting a job or stopped people from talking to me. I've never felt judged by others because of it. Although I'm not proud of my record, I'm not ashamed of where I've been, because where I've been is why I'm where I'm at.

My cousin told me her pastor says our lives are like tapestries. We only see day by day, stitch by stitch. We can't see the ultimate beauty God is weaving. However, if we stand back and look at our lives through God's eyes, we can see the intricate patterns and the relevance of what he's doing in and with and through us.

I gave God every reason to give up on me, yet he still called my name. I'm really thankful. What it comes down to for me is that I know without a doubt Jesus loves me. I'm reminded of that fact every morning when I wake up in a warm house with my wonderful husband and our sweet little baby nearby.

From the time I decided to follow Jesus with all my heart, he's carried me through everything. God blesses faithfulness. He knows when we truly want to follow him, and he makes a way to do it. That's what he's shown me—if I want to follow him, he's always there with me to help me.

Christ used Freedom Fellowship by bringing Shirley into my life, by giving me someone who could teach me how to live. When Christ takes away the desires to use drugs and to steal, he has to replace them with something. Shirley showed me how to live and how to fill the void with God.

I mentor two girls at Turning Point, a girls' residential home in Fort Collins. They are 15 and 17, and were both saved just a few months ago. That's awesome.

We attend 12-step meetings together. I do a one-on-one with each of them every week. Plus, we go out for coffee or soft drinks once a week. They also go to church with us. We spend a lot of time together.

I imagine I'll be working with Turning Point for a long time, because I feel that's what God wants me to do. It's one way I can share the wonderful message of that simple little tract: "Smile, Jesus Loves You."

Chapter 5

God Chooses Nobodies
Angel, Board of Directors

I grew up in the communist state of Bulgaria. When I was 25 years old and a newlywed, I moved to northern Russia to work, because they didn't tax there. I worked for two years in very difficult conditions near the Bering Sea. It wasn't Siberia, but it was almost as severe. I saved most of the money, so my wife and I could buy a car and an apartment in Bulgaria.

When I returned home, we bought a car but not an apartment. God put the thought in my heart: *Don't buy anything. Don't waste your money.*

Then my wife and I started thinking about getting out of Bulgaria. Our son was seven-years old, and our daughter was three. We wanted our children to grow up in a free world. I had grown up in a Christian home. I wanted my children to be able to go to church and freely worship God.

Under the communist rule in Bulgaria, only the leaders were wealthy. Their children went to good schools in France, England and Germany. Ordinary kids had to go to public schools, where they were taught that there is no God. That's not what I wanted for my children.

My wife's brother-in-law, who was Ukrainian, had some people in the Bulgarian Embassy in Moscow send us an invitation to visit them. We could have driven through either Romania or Yugoslavia to get to Moscow. We chose the Yugoslavian route.

Finally, our big day came: June 30, 1981. Our plan was to act like tourists on vacation. When we reached the border between Bulgaria and Yugoslavia, it was 12 noon and very hot. As we drove up, a guard approached us. He moved like a puppet, like he was asleep. I rolled the window down and gave him our passports. He looked at them, looked inside at my family, who also seemed to be asleep, and said, "Go."

When he said, "Go," I drove to the gate. The guard who pushed the buttons to open and close the gate moved puppet-like, the same as the first one. He seemed to be asleep, yet he opened the gate for us, and I drove through.

I know God put those people in that stupor so no one knew how or where we escaped. I'd been to that border many times when I was in the Bulgarian army. Normally, the guards would write down the license number of the car, the registration number, the names of everyone in the vehicle, and more.

The usual procedure for a border crossing was to get out of the car, go inside the guardhouse, and fill out form after form after form listing money, clothing, jewelry, gifts—everything in the car. But all they did was look at our passports and say, "Go." That's unheard of. Only God can do that.

We were so asleep that we don't remember how we got to my aunt's house in Macedonia. I remember driving part of the way, but I have no memory of the rest of the trip. All of a sudden, in a very short time, we found ourselves in front of the building where my aunt lived. I think maybe we were transported.

We learned later that the Bulgarian communists treated my sister and my grandparents, who raised me, very badly after we escaped. They searched their house many times for literature and books—at midnight, at two o'clock in the morning, at three o'clock in the morning.

"Where are the books your son is sending you?" they demanded. My grandparents were old folks. It was very hard on them.

My sister, who was thrown out of school because of our escape, was the most affected. The authorities called her to the police station again and again to interrogate her. Each time, they aimed a bright light at her face and screamed, "Tell us where your brother is!"

She told them over and over, "I don't know. I don't know. He's a grown man with a family. I'm not in control of his life."

Because of our miraculous escape, the police didn't know how we got out of Bulgaria; neither did my family. For six months they had no idea what had happened to us. As far as they knew, we'd gone on vacation and never returned.

One day when I walked out of the American Embassy in Belgrade, the capital of Yugoslavia, a man approached me, saying, "Repent for the kingdom of God is at hand. Repent for the kingdom of God is at hand. Repent for the kingdom of God is at hand."

I wasn't living for the Lord at that time, but I had grown up in a Pentecostal church and loved to talk with people about God. My grandfather planted churches and had visions and encounters with God. He was my hero.

When the man in the square said to repent three times, I was fascinated with his prophecy and decided I would like to talk with him, so I started to approach him. There weren't many people around; yet all of a sudden, the man disappeared.

I looked to the left and to the right and around the square, but he was not there. Years later, when I rededicated my life to Jesus in America, I remembered the man in the Belgrade square. That was the angel of the Lord telling me to repent.

Only one Bulgarian family and one Czech family could be accepted at the American embassy in Yugoslavia. Most escapees told the Americans they wanted to leave for economic reasons. We said we wanted our children to grow up in a free country, and we wanted to worship our God freely.

When the consul came to do a final interview with us, my daughter was sleeping in my wife's arms. He looked at her, smiled, and said, "She doesn't know that in a week she'll be living in the United States of America."

He was a tall man, such a tall American, and he had such a beautiful smile. I thought, *What a guy! He's something else.* But I didn't understand what he said.

"He likes your daughter," the interpreter told me. "He smiles at her."

I said, "There's another reason. I see something different in this man." Looking back, I think he was a Christian. He chose our family because we wanted to go to America so our children could grow up in a free society and so we could freely go to church and freely worship the Lord.

After the final interview at the American embassy, we were told we would be sent to Colorado Springs, Colorado. However, the church that was going to adopt us changed their minds at the last moment. So the Peace of Christ Lutheran Church in Fort Collins sponsored us through the Lutheran offices in New York.

The pastor of the church met us when we arrived in Colorado. We knew only two words in English: "hi" and "thank you." It was hard to adjust to a new country, but God had his purposes for our lives.

After we had been in Fort Collins for some time, I asked one of my colleagues, a Christian, "Where can I find a Pentecostal church around here? My grandfather was a Pentecostal preacher."

He drove me to Resurrection Fellowship after work and said, "Here is a Pentecostal church."

The next Sunday, I attended Resurrection Fellowship. When Pastor John invited people to receive Christ, I rededicated my life to Jesus. My whole family soon accepted Jesus. Later, during special services at the church, prayer was offered for people who wanted to receive the baptism of the Holy Spirit. I went forward with my family for prayer, but nothing happened.

That evening, after my wife and my children went to bed, I received communion alone in the kitchen. I said, "Lord, this is your precious body and blood. I do this in remembrance of who you are."

All of a sudden, the ceiling was filled with tongues of fire, which I sensed and heard but didn't see—thousands of different tongues in the ceiling. I was overwhelmed and ran to the bathroom, where I fell down on my knees.

A tremendous light came over me, and I was baptized by the Holy Ghost with fire. I began speaking in different tongues. They changed every minute, a different one and then a different one.

Afterward, when I entered the bedroom, my wife became frightened. She said, "You're glowing from your waist to the top of your head, like Moses must have glowed after visiting God on the mountain."

We prayed together in the Spirit until three o'clock in the morning. The next day, neither of us felt tired. At work, a coworker from Vietnam said, "What happened to you? You look different!"

That was an awesome, awesome experience, and I have not been the same person since. The power of God changed me so much and put a stamp on me so that I can resist the tricks of the devil and be used for the kingdom of God.

After the fall of Communism in Bulgaria, I returned several times with mission teams from Resurrection Fellowship to witness in the streets and public squares. I also returned to Bulgaria to speak at my grandfather's funeral.

I told the people at the funeral, "When I was a little boy, my grandpa told the Lord, 'This boy belongs to you.' I will continue the work that my grandpa did. He planted churches; I win people for Jesus." I am a soul winner, and I don't apologize for it."

Donna Roth was part of the Resurrection Fellowship team that went into Bulgaria right after Communism fell. Along with others from the church, we performed live dramas, preached, and passed out Gospel tracts. We were able to lead many people to Jesus in the city square right in front of the cultural palace in Sofia.

I was fascinated with the way Donna prayed with people. She always had a heart for others to be baptized in the Holy Spirit. After we returned home from that mission trip, my wife and I began hosting Freedom Fellowship meetings in our home. Donna and the other volunteers came weekly for praise and worship and to pray for the prisons. That's how I became involved with prison ministry.

Donna has such a heart and compassion for people. She's so excited about Jesus, and she cares so much about the prisoners, even those on suicide watch and death row. She goes to them and prays for them, and they get saved and filled with the Holy Spirit.

I started going to prisons with Freedom Fellowship in 1992. My ministry is evangelism. I preach short evangelistic messages then invite people to accept Jesus. That's my calling.

The Holy Spirit empowers me so much that my English improves. God gives me words and utterances to preach his Word and talk straight to the inmates. I tell them, "God knows your touch, he knows your heart. He knows your phone number. He knew your beginning and your end before you were even created. Why are you trying to hide from him? Just repent and surrender." That's what I tell them in prisons.

There is rarely a time that a person is not saved when I evangelize in prison. Because I am straight with the Holy Spirit, the anointing breaks loose and the presence of God is perceptible.

One guy said, "I saw a light like a rainbow around you."

A man in a wheelchair told us that people often rejected him, but he saw something different in us. "If God is as kind and merciful as you say," he said, "then I want him."

It's such a joy for me when a person says "yes" to Jesus. I told that man all the angels of God were lining up right then to sing a song especially composed for him. I said, "Your name is now written in the Lamb's Book of Life."

God uses ordinary people to accomplish his purposes. He chooses nobodies like me and Donna. If God can use us, he can use anybody. Anyone who doesn't think too highly of himself or herself can be used by God. He chooses simple people who are willing and available.

Donna is one of those people. I'm privileged to know a sister who has such a tender heart for lost men and women. I'm fascinated by her simplicity. Her character inspires me to go and help others.

Donna is not perfect. We don't need to put her on a pedestal. Like the prophet Isaiah, Donna said, "I'm available, Lord. Send me," and the Lord sent her. Because she stays in the will of God and relies on the Holy Spirit, God uses her.

Chapter 6

Life Is Good
Andy, Ex-Inmate

My marijuana use began in high school at weekend parties. It wasn't long before I also started partying during the week. I never drank or did hard drugs, but I smoked a lot of pot.

One day, I thought, *Wow, if I grew this stuff, I wouldn't have to pay for it.* By then I was out of school and working full time, so I rented a house, installed hydroponic lights in the basement, and planted some seeds.

When I harvested my first crop, I had plenty of marijuana to smoke and plenty to sell. I rented two more houses with basements. Soon I was making over $100,000 a year growing and selling marijuana.

One weekend I needed to go to a wedding in Chicago, so I paid a friend $300 to stay in the house where I lived. I gave him videos for the VCR. I bought him steaks to cook on the grill. I told him he could go to school, go out, whatever. All he had to do was sleep there. I just wanted him to be there at night and to make sure my dog had food and water.

As soon as I left, he opened up the sliding glass doors for the dog and took off for the weekend. My dog ate all the food and drank all the water, then started barking. Eventually, my neighbor called the police.

The cops knocked on the front door. No one answered, so they went around to the backyard, where they saw that the door was open. They went inside to see if everything was all right, to make sure no one was sick or hurt.

That's when they found the marijuana. It must have been God's timing, because it certainly wasn't mine. I was all set, had covered all my bases, I thought. I got the news at the rehearsal dinner in Chicago, when the host walked up and said, "Mr. Taggart, you have a phone call."

I took the call and heard a friend say, "Andy, I drove by your house today. Police tape is wrapped all around it."

The moment I returned home, I hired an attorney. He called the police department almost every day for a year, asking, "Is there a warrant out for Andy yet?" When they finally put the warrant out, I immediately turned myself in.

But I was let off on a deferred sentence, which is nothing. If they had put me in jail back then, a month would have been enough to wake me up. However, I didn't spend even a day behind bars, so my life continued on as it was. I actually kept growing pot. If they had pulled me out of my life and set me in jail for long enough to make me think about what I was doing, things might have been different.

I was given a four-year deferred sentence and did around 400 hours of community service. Things were going great until I was charged with trespassing when I tried to collect from a friend who owed me money. Thinking the charge was no big deal, I moved to Connecticut.

I wasn't trying to escape. I just wanted to live with my mom and work a couple jobs, so I could save up some money. I'd finally had enough of growing pot.

By that time, I was the father of a toddler named Amber, whose mother wouldn't let me visit her. I needed to make money to deal with the trespassing charge and to pursue the visitation process with my daughter.

Although I didn't realize it, I wasn't supposed to leave Colorado due to the charge pending against me. Before I was able to get established in Connecticut, I was arrested. The authorities thought I was running from the law. They considered me to be a fugitive and decided to extradite me to Colorado.

I was packed into the back of a small van that contained nine other prisoners and two drivers. Our feet were shackled. Our handcuffed wrists were tied to our waists. We were fed twice a day—an Egg McMuffin at 6 a.m. and a McDonald's hamburger at 6 p.m. That was it.

The trip to Colorado took two long weeks. We were not once allowed to shower, change our clothes, or brush our teeth. Needless to say, we were 10 very stinky men crammed together inside a very smelly van.

The only time we got out of the car was to use the bathrooms at rest stops, which wasn't often. When people saw us hobbling into the restrooms, they'd glance at our chains, grab their children, and run to their vehicles. It was awful. On top of all that, before we climbed back into the van, the drivers sprayed each of us with Lysol.

Six days after we left Connecticut, we returned there to pick up another fugitive. The drivers grabbed a guy in Pennsylvania on Tuesday and one in Ohio on Thursday. Back and forth they drove, just wandering around collecting fugitives. They evidently wanted to fit as many people as they could into the van before heading to Colorado.

We sat upright 24 hours a day. The radio was always on and always tuned to stations that played mariachi music. Mariachi is fine once in a while, but at top volume 24 hours a day, it was torture. We didn't stop to sleep at motels. We just kept going for two weeks, night and day.

In Pennsylvania, the drivers left us sitting in the van for 10 or 11 hours while they visited with relatives. In Denver, they left us in the van in a pitch-dark underground garage for 18 hours. Every now and then, they came down to take us to a bathroom, but they didn't feed us. By the time we arrived in Fort Collins, the Larimer County Detention Center looked like paradise, and my cast-iron bed felt like a cloud.

I knew I had messed up my life, and I was curious about Christianity, so I started talking to God. *Lord, please help me here. Please show me what this is all about. Why are so many people who are into you so happy? What are you all about? My mom is into you. My grandmother was really into you. What am I missing here?*

It bothered me a lot to not be around Amber. I had no idea where she was, what she was doing, whether or not she was healthy. She was less than two-years old at the time.

I prayed fervently that God would communicate to my daughter that I loved her, and that I was not away from her because I wanted to be. I didn't know any way on this earth to give her that assurance, so I asked God comfort her and let her know.

For two or three months I prayed all day every day, *Please, please, Lord, communicate to Amber that I love her.* One night, I woke up in the middle of the night knowing without a doubt that God had answered my prayers. I said, "Thank you, Lord," turned over, and went back to sleep.

That moment was also the answer to my questions: "Why are people so interested in you? Are you for real?" The fact that he heard and answered my prayers was proof enough to me that he was real, and that he loved me, even though I was incarcerated.

I started studying the Bible and going to church services at the jail. Then I heard that the chaplain, Donna Roth, was very nice and helpful, so I had a chat with her. She prayed with me and gave me 10 or 15 Bible verses to study pertaining to my situation.

The good thing about LCDC is that 15 to 20 churches send in people every week to do services. There was nothing else to do in jail, and I was real interested in what they had to offer, so I went to every service, four or five church services a day. It was great. We got to sing and pray and fellowship.

We also had prayer groups of 25, 30, 35 men that met every night. Twenty percent of the inmates in LCDC participated in the prayer circles while I was there.

I could see what Christianity was doing for other people. A guy would come in looking like a wreck, and I could watch his growth. In a short time, he'd be all cleaned up, reading the Bible and joining the Bible studies. He would also participate in the worship time instead of just standing there listening during the singing. And soon he would be trying to spread Christianity to other people.

One day, I said to Donna, "I want to get baptized." So she lined it up. Then she suggested I be baptized with the Holy Spirit. After she showed me some verses on Holy Spirit baptism, I said, "OK, let's do it."

From jail, I went on to prison. When I first got there, it seemed like everyone was in gangs—fighting, doing tattoos, doing drugs—just up to no good. One of the worst things about imprisonment is that many of the inmates have no desire to better themselves in any way. Plus, they want to beat up those who do try to change.

An exception to that mindset was a black man who was about 70 years old. Every day, I saw him sitting at a table studying for his GED. *Wow,* I thought, *this guy is actually trying to do something, when everyone else is doing nothing.*

Finally, I sat down and talked with him. He said, "I'm having a hard time with the algebra."

"I'm pretty good at algebra," I told him. "I'll help you." So I tutored him, but the Nazis didn't like it. They harassed me in the hallways, called me names, cut in front of me in the lunch line, blew in my ear—little irritations every day just to bother and annoy me.

I didn't know what to do. *Do I start swinging? Do I tell somebody?* I didn't want to be a rat and get beat up, so I just let it be for a few weeks. But one day I started yelling, and they backed off a little bit.

The guy I was tutoring told his "brothers" to watch my back. Suddenly, I had all these guys who were doing life without parole coming up to me and saying, "Hey, man, what do you want me to do?"

"Everything all right, man?"

They'd pat me on the back. "Anything I can do for you?"

"Want me to go shank that guy?"

"No, no," I quickly responded. "Everything is okay right now. If I need help, I'll let you know."

My friend also talked with the leader of the Ku Klux Klan and told him to tell his boys to back off. Things mellowed out after that.

In prison, I built on what I had learned about God while in jail. I did a Bible correspondence course, 25 or so books. I read each book, did tests, sent them in, and got back certificates of completion. I learned a lot from those lessons. They were just the basic stories in the Bible, but the course went into detail on each one.

After I was released, I spent a year in the Halfway House. I left there almost two years ago then wore an ankle bracelet for a year. When that was removed, I started my parole. It's a slow, grueling process. I still have another year and a half of parole time.

I no longer have a desire for marijuana, not even close. I wouldn't give up my new life for anything. I have the Lord, I'm able to spend a little time with my daughter, I'm part of a neat church, and the painting business I started a few months ago is going great.

On top of all that, I just married a wonderful woman named Christine. Donna Roth performed the ceremony. Life is good, thanks to what God and Freedom Fellowship have done for me.

Chapter 7

The Mountain of Prison
Sarah and Mandy, Inmates

(Sarah)

I have been a Christian since I was 12 or 13 years old, but I backslid and got into trouble. Although I've come back to God, I still struggle with a lot of temptations and trials. Freedom Fellowship lifts my spirits and gives me guidance.

The way the Freedom Fellowship speaker talks about God is so inspiring for me. The word pictures he paints are ones that stay with me for a long, long time. They make me want to keep striving for God more. He brings out the humor and the pain of life, everything a person needs to recognize about our lives and how we should live for Christ.

The music is great. And the worship leaders are always so enthusiastic. They teach us new and different songs each time.

We receive attendance certificates from Freedom Fellowship. Those are neat. They're nice for our own remembrances and also so others can see how we're trying to become better Christians. When we apply for sentence reductions or parole, the certificates are helpful. Our advisors like to see us participating in self-improvement seminars.

Ginny has been a blessing to me. When I came to my first Freedom Fellowship seminar, she sat down with me and prayed with me. I told her about my little girl and some other concerns. It helped me so much to have her pray for me and comfort me.

Hearing her words of encouragement to keep striving and working things out has helped me. Just to hear someone say everything is going to be okay makes me feel better. Freedom Fellowship doesn't come very often, but Ginny always remembers my name and my kids' names.

(Mandy)

I grew up going to church, but I had many dysfunctions and have been an incredible failure in my life. I've been incarcerated for over four years, since I was 19 years old. I have a 53-years-to-life sentence.

Before I arrived, my idea of prison was that inmates deserved what they got because they committed a crime. They certainly didn't deserve pampering. Possibly, they should have food and warmth. I've learned differently on the inside.

I've also learned that jailhouse religion is okay. The book of Matthew says Jesus came for the sinners. God comes to prison, because that's where the sinners are. No wonder people find Christ in jail; that's where he is, with the sinful and the weak. I believe very few people fake religion in prison. Most of the time they are sincere, just like sick people in hospitals.

A person doesn't have much of an escape in prison, or much of a life. It's easy to get into a survivor mode when you're incarcerated. Most inmates just watch TV or read books. And they trade their illegal addictions for legal ones like sugar and caffeine.

I've recently realized that with God we can have something more than mere existence. I decided several months ago that the way to live the Christian life is to let God take care of me one day at a time. I'm learning to enjoy each day and not be in survivor mode.

I've also come to realize that life is not about me. It's about Jesus, and my hope is stayed on him through whatever. He'll let me out when he's ready. In the meantime, I'll live each day for him. That's where my hope is.

Right now, I'm asking God to help me to not let prison come between us. Everything in my life becomes an issue when I try to see God through the mountain of prison. I want to be able to see God clearly and to say, "Okay, mountain, here's my God." I live for God, or I die.

When Freedom Fellowship volunteers come to minister to us, everything said builds up my heart and my spirit. Their enthusiasm is encouraging. I believe it's not the people who come in here who impact us; it's the Holy Spirit, it's God. I pray God will prepare the prison every time religious seminars are scheduled, and I invite the Holy Spirit to be here.

A person's house may look nice on the outside, but sometimes it's not habitable on the inside. That's the way my life was. I've gone through a demolition, and I'm in the process of rebuilding.

The foundation I had my house built on was faulty. Through the ministry of Freedom Fellowship and others, God has given me a new faith and a new hope—something better, something anointed. I have a new peace. I'm not as sad and brokenhearted as I was before. I'm a changed woman.

My life would be hopeless without the Lord. I could not make it without having a relationship with him. I need God more than anything in life, more than any of my wants or desires, even my desire to get out of prison.

Chapter 8

No More "Buts"

Harold, Inmate

In 1978, when I was a teenager, my family traveled from Colorado to California for Christmas vacation. After we'd been there a few days, my cousin asked me to go to church with her the next night.

I said, "If you go to Knott's Berry Farm with us in the morning, I'll go to church with you at night."

She agreed but became ill and couldn't go with us to Knott's Berry Farm, so I didn't feel obligated to go to church with her, even though she felt better. Despite my argument, she stayed on my case.

Finally, I said, "Okay, okay. I'll go with you." I grabbed my bag of drugs, rode to church with her, and got high during the service.

When the pastor finished preaching, he had us bow our heads. "If you want to accept Jesus," he said, "raise your hand." I was sitting on my hands, thinking there was no way they were going up. But all of a sudden, one hand popped up, like it had a mind of its own.

Then he said, "Open your eyes, please. I'd like those of you who raised your hands to walk to the front and voice that decision."

I figured nobody had seen me raise my hand, so I wasn't going forward. No way. Besides, I was higher than high, and I knew it.

Just as all those thoughts were racing through my mind, my cousin reached over and put her hand on my knee. Instantly, I jumped up and ran to the front of the sanctuary, tears flowing, and gave my life to Jesus. I even flushed all the drugs in my bag down a toilet at the church. On the way home, we stopped at an ice cream parlor to celebrate. Life was good.

For the next year and a half, I grew spiritually strong and close to God. I lived my life for him every step I took and made plans to go to New Guinea with Teen Missions to build an airstrip. However, the day before I was supposed to leave, God told me plans had changed. I was not going with Teen Missions.

After all the preparation and raising all the necessary funds, I forfeited the trip. But, because I did, on January 2, 1979, I was able to see my whole family come to the Lord—my sister, my mother and my dad. My dad was an alcoholic at that time and has been sober ever since.

During the following years, I followed God off and on but got sidetracked by drugs over and over again. My father doesn't understand my addiction to cocaine. He was delivered immediately from alcohol—never had another craving. With me, I get into Christianity and walk with God for a while, then I start thinking I can do it on my own. Every time I do that, I fall flat on my face.

I believe God has allowed me to live my life the way I've lived it to build a testimony, even with all the bad choices I've made. I can tell those involved in drugs: "I've done time for my drugs. I've done time for my crimes. If you want to end up like me, keep doing what you're doing."

I've been incarcerated again and again. I destroyed a 17-year marriage to a wonderful woman. I lost good jobs, a new house, and a new car. I even attempted suicide. My calling is to share my story with others, so they don't ruin their lives like I did mine.

My battle with cocaine came to a head early in 1996, when I asked my wife what she wanted for her 40th birthday. Carla was an enabler and a co-dependent person, who didn't want to live alone, but my addiction had come to the point where she couldn't take it any longer.

She told me she wanted me out of her life, that she wanted me to get help, and she wanted me to leave her alone. My addictive lifestyle was killing her. I walked out the door with my torch and my pipe and our credit cards, with which I immediately purchased a half ounce of cocaine.

In the next six months I dropped $65,000 in cocaine. I also received three DUI's during that time period. Finally, at 12:30 in the morning, on June 8, 1996, standing in the rain in Denver's Washington Park, I picked up a pay phone and called the cocaine hotline. I told the lady who answered that I needed help.

She talked with me a bit. After learning that I had not failed an out-patient program, that I had not been appointed by the courts, and that I had no insurance, she decided I did not have a cocaine problem. I put the phone down and hit the pipe again. I could hear her voice calling, "Sir? Sir, are you there?"

After I let out my hit, I picked up the phone.

The woman said, "What did you just do?"

71

I responded, "Since I don't have a problem, I might as well finish what I started. If you don't hear from me in the morning, you'll read about me in the newspaper."

The next day, I called my folks and told them they needed to come and get me. "Otherwise," I said, "I'll soon be in a box six-feet under, because I'm ready to end it all."

When my parents picked me up, I weighed 92 pounds. My mom says I looked like "death walking." Later, when she showed me pictures she'd taken of me at that time, I didn't recognize myself. I was in bad shape.

Eventually, I was arrested and jailed. Carla came to the court hearing with my grandparents. The judge was about to sentence me back to probation when Carla stood, explained who she was, and asked if she could address the court. The judge nodded his head.

"Your Honor," she said, her voice shaking, "Harold has spent $65,000 on cocaine in the last six months, all of it charged on our credit cards. He told me that the credit card companies will have to catch him to get any money out of him. He says he isn't going to pay them because he doesn't need to pay them."

The judge looked at me and asked if it was true. I said, "I'm in orange. She's in street clothes. You believe who you want." I was furious.

He said, "I will not have a mockery made of my court. I sentence you to six months in jail." Then he told me to sit down. As I sat, I turned and glared at Carla, as angry as can be. But in her eyes, I saw a look of love and pain I will never forget.

When the guards returned me to my cell that afternoon and slammed the door behind me, I was so angry that all I could do was pound the floor and scream. After I came to my senses and calmed down, I realized that the six-month sentence was the best gift Carla could ever give me. I *had* to clean up. I couldn't use drugs any longer.

Another day on the streets would have killed me. Even though Carla was in the process of divorcing me, she cared enough to go to court and ask the judge to put me back in jail. She loved me enough to save my life.

My recent association with Larimer County Detention Center, Community Corrections, and Freedom Fellowship is a result of an April 1st arrest. I was headed to Las Vegas for a vacation and then to Montana to run bootleg and stolen goods off a reservation. The woman I was traveling with was leaving her husband in Colorado. Her family in Montana ran the outlaw company.

We rented a motel room in Fort Collins. The cops came to the front door. We walked out the back door of the motel. First strike.

On the way down to the Denver airport, we were stopped by the state patrol, because we didn't make a complete stop at a stop sign as we left a liquor store. The patrolman could have run a driver's license check on us but didn't, for some reason. That was the second strike.

When we got to Denver, our flight to Vegas was delayed, so we rented a hotel room for the night. I ordered a pizza and was told it would take an hour and ten minutes. An hour went by. I smoked a joint, opened a bottle of alcohol, and poured myself a drink.

Then I heard a knock on the door. I looked through the peephole but didn't see anything but a thumb print. I figured the pizza guy was goofing around and opened the door to find myself face to face with three uniformed police officers. Their guns were drawn, and the big dogs at their sides were poised for attack.

"Good evening," said one officer. "We have a warrant for your arrest."

I laughed. "This is an April Fool's joke, right?"

"No, sir," he answered. "The joke is on you. You're going to jail."

I later learned that those officers comprised a task force that does nothing but run warrants through Denver hotel registries. My warrant was for violation of probation in Larimer County. I was on probation for driving while under suspension, but I wasn't aware of the warrant. Strike three. I soon found myself headed back to Fort Collins and the Larimer County Detention Center.

I knew I had to change, so I started going to the jail church services and Bible studies. One day when I walked into a service, there were cards on the chairs that read "One-Way Ticket." The leader for that session asked us to write on the card what we wanted God to do for us.

I wrote "No More Buts" on mine, because so many times I give a problem to God but don't let go completely. The leader said she wanted us to pray over the ticket when we got back to our rooms and to trust God that it would come to pass. Then she suggested we tear up the paper and flush it down the toilet, which would be a symbolic way of releasing the situation and not being able to take it back. "No More Buts" has been my theme song ever since.

Despite my determination to change, I received three write-ups in a matter of a week and was sent to "the hole" for eight days. The hole is a solitary cell where an inmate is let out for only one hour a day—half an hour for recreation time, 15 minutes for a shower, 15 minutes for phone calls. The other 23 hours he's in his cell with just a book and possibly a notepad. I read the entire New Testament in those eight days.

When I finished my time, I was supposed to go back to my original pod. But I was told that the segregation had changed, and I would have to stay in the holding cell until an opening came up.

Well, after eight days, I was going batty without someone to talk to. I spoke with one of the guards about my situation. He said, "Let me see what I can do." An hour-and-a-half later, he came back, saying, "Pack your stuff up. You're going to another pod."

I walked into the pod and saw a guy I'd met at the Bible studies who was on fire for God. He was such an inspiration and such a motivator, even though he was looking at a life sentence for attempted murder.

He had lost his job, his wife, his kids, and an induction to the state wrestling hall of fame; yet, he kept praising God. I was touched because, despite his discouraging fate, he gave it all to God.

I'd been praying there would be somebody in my new pod I could minister to or who could minister to me. Well, this guy's name was Mark, and I was placed in his cell. It was such a blessing for me.

Mark and I prayed before breakfast. After breakfast, we went back to our cell and prayed most of the morning. We also prayed during lockdowns at 11:00 a.m., 4:00 p.m., and 10:30 p.m. Every time we went into the room, we prayed.

When you walked into our cell, God's presence was there, because we claimed the room for Jesus. We also started a Bible study in our pod. Every evening at 10:00, up to 18 guys joined together in a prayer circle. Soon, each one of the pods had a similar group. It wasn't long before nearly everyone in the jail was praying at the same time each night. What a unity we experienced.

Mark and I started believing a miracle was going to take place in his life. On the first of July, he got a phone call from his mother. She said a man whose son Mark had taught to wrestle had called and said God had laid it on his heart to find out what Mark needed.

Mark's bond was $150,000. There was no way he could come up with that kind of money. However, he he'd just gone to a hearing where his bond had been dropped to $75,000. This man, who happened to be the president of a bank in Pueblo, said to Mark's mother, "You call Mark and tell him to pack his bags, because I'm sending a check for $75,000, so he can get out."

That was on the 1st of July. The bondsman was supposed to come to the jail at 3:30 that afternoon. But he went to Denver and didn't make it on the 1st. The 2nd of July came. Nothing happened. July 3rd came and went. Still nothing.

We just kept believing God that Mark was going to get out. On the 4th of July, we got all excited and thought that would be the date of his return to freedom. Well, the 4th passed by, but Mark still continued to praise God that a miracle was on the way.

When we returned from church on the 5th, Mark went into our cell, and I sat down at a table in the commons area to play cards. About 1:45 in the afternoon, a guard came in and asked where Mark was.

I looked up. "Why?" I asked. "Is he going home?"

The guard stared at me kind of funny then said, "How did you know?"

"God said Mark was going to go home," I replied. "It was just a matter of his timing." The guard just looked at me.

I went running into the cell. Mark was down on his knees beside his bunk praying in tongues. I tapped him on the shoulder and told him to pack his bags—he was going home. He jumped up and we both started crying and hugging each other and praising God. Our prayers had been answered.

Mark's departure was bittersweet for me, but I knew I had to move on with my own life. Freedom Fellowship helped. The volunteers who came to minister to us at LCDC treated us with kindness and love, even though we were in orange and behind bars. It didn't matter to them. They had such compassionate hearts that they treated us like individuals, like brothers and sisters.

I was especially touched by Pastor Dave. Here was a man who could have been home spending time with his family, but he chose to come in and share the Word with us. Not only did I find a pastor while I was in jail, I found a friend and a brother in Christ. He's truly a man of God.

For many, many years, I was in denial about my cocaine habit. With the help of God and Freedom Fellowship, I've finally came to the point where I admit I have an addiction. Although I realize I have a problem with drugs, I also know that the old person has died, and a new one has been born through God's forgiveness, love and grace.

When I come out of this, Satan had better watch out. I'm coming out with both barrels loaded, and I plan to take back the ground he's stolen from me.

Chapter 9

Just Love Them
Debbie and Bart, Board of Directors

(Bart)

O ur association with Freedom Fellowship began when I overheard a conversation between two women standing in the Resurrection Fellowship church foyer. They were talking about ministering to inmates at the Larimer County Detention Center. I heard one of them say the ministry had a critical need for Bibles because so many men and women in the jail wanted to study the Word and learn more about Jesus Christ. At that moment, I felt a tremendous urge, or leading of the Holy Spirit—not a voice, but a leading to give them some money so they could buy Bibles and carry on with what they were doing at the jail.

From that point on, Debbie and I became more and more involved with Freedom Fellowship. We started helping conduct the Friday night Bible studies at the jail. We were able to meet the inmates, pray with them, and encourage them.

I began to counsel inmates who expressed a desire to talk and pray with a volunteer concerning their future and their faith. Those counseling sessions tremendously strengthened my own relationship with the Lord. I saw miracles happen. I experienced the Holy Spirit speaking to me and to the men. I saw lives changed. My wife and I were able to watch men leave the detention center and go on to lead wholesome, productive lives.

I also visited the Halfway House to talk to inmates living at that facility. Sometimes the residents struggle to meet the demands of Community Corrections. It can be a difficult time for them. I was there to encourage and counsel them.

Years ago, when Freedom Fellowship was first formed, I was asked to join the board of directors. As a board member, I assisted in various logistical functions, like obtaining a tax-exempt status for the ministry and recognition as a charitable institution by the state of Colorado. I've also been involved in the fund-raising aspect of the ministry. Although Debbie and I now serve in another ministry organization, we are both on the Freedom Fellowship board.

I continue to assist Freedom Fellowship as a board member because I'm selfish. I want to be close to God, whose heart is in jail with the inmates. Prisoners are heavy on his heart. I want to work where he's working.

(Debbie)

When we first met Donna, she kept telling us about this wonderful ministry in the prisons and how God was moving and touching people's lives, how he was changing and healing them. She kept drawing us in. "Why don't you come in with us sometime?" she asked, again and again.

Finally, I went to jail with her. I remember standing in the hallway at LCDC feeling a bit nervous. I'd never before been inside a jail. I didn't know anybody in jail. I didn't know what to expect. I didn't know what to say.

I remember asking Donna, "What do I say? What should I do? What's going to happen?"

She turned, looked at me, and said three words: "Just love them." Those three words changed my life. It was as if Jesus was speaking to me. All of a sudden, I realized how simple it is to minister to hurting people. When she told me to *just love them*, I felt peace come over me. I thought, *That's easy. I can do that.*

We tend to assume we need to go to Bible school or be great, anointed preachers to be able to minister to people. But, it's just a matter of loving others where they are and letting God speak through us to touch their hearts.

I went into the jail Bible study with Donna, and I loved it. God was so apparent there. I saw his grace and his compassion and his love being revealed. Going to jail or traveling to prison soon became one of the highlights of my week.

Bart and I began to lead the Friday night service at LCDC. Bart counseled, and I taught and led praise and worship, along with a couple other volunteers. We had a wonderful time with the inmates.

During our years of volunteering with Freedom Fellowship, we saw hundreds of inmates become Christians. People came to the Lord at every meeting. Some may not have been serious about it or had true conversions, but with most of them, you could see an immediate change in their faces. Suddenly, they'd have tears and big smiles, and I would think, *Salvation is the greatest miracle of all.*

We were privileged to see those instantaneous transformations and to watch inmates continue with the Bible studies and grow in their relationships with God. At weekend prison seminars, we'd get to encourage those we'd met at LCDC to continue to walk with the Lord.

Volunteering changed our lives as much as it did theirs. I can remember Bart coming home teary-eyed, saying, "You have to hear what God did tonight!"

It's wonderful to go to church and hear a good message and praise God. But when you see God work through you to change lives that look so hopeless, it transforms your own life and helps you see who Jesus really is. That experience is something people miss when they just sit in the pew on Sunday morning. Never in church have I seen Jesus in the fullness I've seen him in prison.

After my first experience at LCDC, God told me, "I am sending you to people nobody wants, not even my church, but I love them." He gave us the ability to see their hearts, to see them as made in the image of God. We didn't focus on their sin or the crimes they'd committed. We saw how Satan had destroyed their lives, often from the time they were little children.

Many of them began living on the streets at young ages after they were kicked out of their homes. Their parents were alcoholics, on drugs, or just didn't want to take care of them. God showed us his compassion for them and his desire to see them restored to what he had planned for their lives.

The inmates have told us they sense the love and the presence of the Lord at the seminars as well as the freedom to express their worship to God. Their lives are touched by the Lord. It's not about Freedom Fellowship feeding their minds with information but about helping them come into heart-to-heart contact with God. We want to expose them to the love of God and the reality of Jesus.

I remember a prison seminar where we divided into small groups to discuss what the speaker had talked about. We went around the circle and asked each individual to share his thoughts. One man sat there stone-faced, his arms folded. He refused to say anything and did not want to be a part of the discussion. He just sat there looking at us like we were crazy.

I wondered, *Why are you here? Nobody forced you to come to this seminar.*

Afterward, during the cookie-and-coffee time, I went over to talk with him. I wanted to find out why he seemed so closed. We talked for a while. Then I asked him, "Do you know Jesus?"

He said, "I would have to see him standing here to believe he is real."

I felt faith rise up in my heart and found myself saying, "That's not hard. God is able to reveal himself to you. Let's pray."

We bowed our heads. I prayed, "God, please reveal yourself to this man."

The next day, right before the Saturday morning meeting, that same man came running up to me. "You'll never guess what happened!" he exclaimed. "Last night after the meeting, I was sitting on my bunk, and all of a sudden, Jesus came into my cell. I didn't see him with my eyes, but I felt his presence, like warm water being poured over me. Jesus was there, and I knew it. He was so wonderful I couldn't resist him. Please pray with me. I want him in my life."

That experience showed me God is able to meet us wherever we are, even if we have no faith. He's able to reveal himself to us. What I prayed was just a short, simple, honest prayer. I think God enjoys honesty.

My friend was totally transformed by seeing Jesus. His demeanor and his desires were changed. He was almost drunk with God's love. Before that transformation, he was the hardest man I'd ever talked with.

We had other instances where the Holy Spirit was so strong in our meetings, the guards joined us. They wanted to be part of what was going on. Although the chapels were packed with inmates, the guards squeezed in among them. Many people were healed and changed forever. Those were times we'll never forget.

At one prison, after I had taught two services, the Lord said to me, *I want you to study the glory of God.* So I studied it that night. However, when I got to the prison the next morning, I had a sense that I would not do much teaching.

During the worship time I talked a little about God's glory and how nothing stays the same when it comes. Suddenly, the glory of God came down, and the meeting room was filled with his presence. Two of the inmates ran out of the room. They couldn't handle his glory.

I felt led to call people up who wanted more of God. Men began to come to the front, shaking all over, and falling on the floor. One man began to speak loudly in tongues. Another inmate came forward with an interpretation of the tongues. It was right on, an exact confirmation of what God was doing.

Silently, I asked God to hide the commotion from the guards. I feared they might frown on the unusual happenings in that room. We had quite a time that morning, and God faithfully covered our activities.

I'll never forget one man who came up. He was huge—must have been 6 foot 5 inches, maybe taller, with big, bulging muscles. All he said was, "I want more of God," and the fire of God hit him, just like that. He started shaking so hard that two of the guys had to hold him up. Sweat dripped down his whole body. He was literally in the fire of God.

I prayed, "Give him more of yourself, Lord. Give him more."

He stood there for 20 minutes shaking and burning up. I sensed God's fire was purifying him, burning the dross out of him. Afterward, he had a beautiful, peaceful expression on his face.

Then another man came running up, shouting, "I'm healed, I'm healed!" He was just sitting in his chair, and God healed him of chronic stomach pain. It was the most amazing time.

I ended the service by saying, "This is what the glory of God is."

That was all I needed to say. Jesus had demonstrated his love and power. The most important thing in any ministry is to lead people into the presence of God and then let him do whatever he wants to do.

Years ago, we had Freedom Fellowship prayer meetings at our home every Thursday evening. One night when we finished praying for the inmates and the ministry, Donna felt led to go around the room to pray for each person and prophesy about them. When she came to me, she prophesied that God was going to use me to reach his people, Israel. Soon after that, I traveled to Russia with a Christian Jewish lady to visit Jewish families who were being persecuted by the government.

Before the fall of Communism, our work had to be done in a clandestine manner. The Russian phones were bugged, the rooms were bugged, the hotels were bugged.

Everything we did had to be done in code and directed by the Holy Spirit.

Because I'd learned through prison and jail ministry to be led by the Spirit, I let God show me where to go, what to say, and what to do. It was like a James Bond spiritual undercover mission, but God was with us. We ministered to 27 Jewish families in Moscow and St. Petersburg who were being pressured by the government because of their Jewishness.

Not long after that first trip, Bart and I were asked to work with the Ebenezer Emergency Fund, which was an international ministry that helped Russian Jews immigrate out of Russia to Israel. We worked as the United States coordinators for that endeavor.

Now we lead a ministry called Preparing the Way that helps North American Jews return to Israel. We also teach Christians about their Biblical call to love and support Israel and the Jewish people. I believe God trained us in the prison ministry for the work we do now.

I learned so much about walking in the Spirit from Donna Roth and Freedom Fellowship. I learned that God is with me, that he will protect me and give me grace to do his work. I can do anything he asks of me, if I trust him.

Chapter 10

Giving Back
Art, Ex-Inmate

In Colton, California, where I grew up, a kid had to belong to a gang in order to survive. Although I was never initiated into a gang, I hung out with a couple of groups from South Colton. Most of the time we were peaceful, but we occasionally had conflicts with other gangs.

I started drinking, smoking pot and doing drugs when I was 15 or 16. I got into trouble with the law a few times for misdemeanors, but I straightened out when I joined the Marine Corps at age 17. The Marines taught me discipline.

They also taught me to be swift, silent and deadly, and how to enter and leave buildings without being detected. They taught me how to steal, kill, destroy and sabotage the enemy. I applied those lessons later on in my criminal activities, which was exciting to me, because I didn't get to see much action during the Vietnam War.

By the time I was discharged from the Marine Corps in 1977, I was married and had a little girl named Tina. My wife and I decided to move to Colorado, where I found work doing construction. Some months were slow, so I got involved with criminal activities to make ends meet. It wasn't long before we had a second child, a son we called J.R.

I also played with different bands in the bars at night and sold drugs on the side. Eventually, my lifestyle destroyed my family. My wife and I divorced in 1982. When we split up, I went wild.

Then I met a woman from Cheyenne, Wyoming. We had a little girl together, Chasity, and we all moved to California. Things didn't work out in the relationship, so my girlfriend left and took Chasity with her. I stayed on the West Coast selling drugs and living crazy on the streets.

After about four years of that, I decided to move back to Colorado to be close to my kids. Both my ex-wife and ex-girlfriend were living there with my children. I found work, but I also sold crystal methamphetamine and marijuana, did robberies and continued playing music in the bars. As a result, I neglected my children.

One day when I needed money in a hurry, I decided to rob a former employer. I had a personal vendetta against him, because he owed me money. A friend helped me, and we emptied his business. We took everything he had, stripped the place right down to the floor.

My plan was to wipe him out, sell his stuff, and not get caught. But the Lord had different plans. Shortly after our robbery, police officers searched my co-thief's apartment regarding another matter and found some of my former employer's tools, which were still engraved with the company name.

My friend had secretly slipped them into his pocket as we were doing the robbery. The cops grilled him. He talked. I heard over my scanner that the authorities were looking for me, so I stayed away for a few days. But they eventually caught up with me and arrested me. I was actually arrested five or six times for seven or eight different felonies and charged with crimes I knew nothing about. That was because my brother-in-law tried to help me by selling the stuff I stole to a guy in Loveland, who sold it to someone else. Those guys were all involved with drugs.

The authorities found an ice chest full of cocaine along with the items I had stolen. They also found tools and other things I was not responsible for. The list got longer and longer. Before I knew it, I had several felony charges against me. In the end, I was charged with two felonies. They planned to give me 20 years because of the amount of money involved. They also arrested my wife, my brother-in-law, my sister-in law, and other people close to me.

When they arrested my wife, who had nothing to do with the robbery, that was the last straw for me. My lawyer talked with the district attorney, and we plea-bargained for an eight-year sentence and a four-year sentence to be served through Community Corrections.

That wasn't too bad. However, after nine months at the Halfway House, I violated Community Corrections and was sent to the Larimer County Detention Center. As they closed the cell door behind me, I landed on my knees. I remember crying out to God, telling him, "I surrender. I want to serve You." I knew he was calling me to leave my wild ways.

I met Donna Roth at LCDC. She was a wonderful mentor to me. She prayed with me and gave me Scriptures, just like she does with many of the inmates. She touched my heart and was a big part of my salvation, a big part of my walk with God, my spiritual growth.

The judge gave me concurrent eight-year and four-year prison sentences and the option for reconsideration. I left LCDC and was transferred through several different prisons over the next few years. Along the way, I served the Lord and read the Word of God. The Bible came to life for me. Everything I read in Scripture came to life. I had to act it out. I had to confront all my issues.

Prison is a good place to get strong in your faith and to prepare yourself for the outside world, because it can be real tough at times. God told me I would do prison ministry when I got out and that I would also minister with music.

At Buena Vista and Canyon City, I wrote songs in my head, without the aid of an instrument. The prison at Rifle had instruments, so when I got there, I could play my songs. I joined the chapel worship team and was assigned to be a chaplain's assistant, which enabled me to be in the Word most the time.

Sixteen other inmates were processed into Rifle the same weekend I was. Every one of them was a Christian brother. I believe the Lord put us together for a reason. They were all prayer warriors, very strong in the Word, knowledgeable and committed to serving God.

At that time, a dark cloud seemed to hover over the town of Rifle. Several satanic cults were active in the city, and the churches were being emptied. Somebody in Rifle heard a word from God that there were 17 inmates at the prison who were really strong prayer warriors and who were supposed to pray for the city.

Our chaplain told us, "The city of Rifle is crying out. They know God has put 17 of you here to pray for this city." So we got together and started praying.

All 17 of us fasted and prayed for an entire week. On the last day, Saturday, we crowded together in a small room and held hands and prayed. I don't know how long we prayed; it must have been for hours.

While we were praying, God literally jolted that place. The whole complex trembled with his presence. It felt like he was taking the camp and shaking the demons out of it.

We all sensed the presence of the Lord, and we all felt the buildings quake. It reminded me of that passage in the New Testament where God shook the prison Paul and Silas were in and opened the doors.

Prison is loud. Televisions blare, the P.A. system blasts instructions, people yell and cuss and throw things. That's just the way prison is. It's very chaotic.

But when we stopped praying, it was so quiet you could hear a pin drop. Most of the guards and inmates had exited the building when it started to shake. The five or six men left inside joined us in chapel the next morning to give their lives to God.

Each of the 17 prayer warriors was a first-phase inmate, who would not normally have been permitted to leave the facility. However, all of us were allowed to go into the city of Rifle, to tell them what had happened, give our testimonies, and pray for the churches. We also shared several of the songs I wrote. Some churches had only a few members left. Over time, as we continued to pray, pews began to fill again.

Another highlight of my imprisonment happened when my oldest daughter, Tina, gave her life to the Lord through my letters. She wrote and asked me questions about the Bible and about God, and I answered them. I was overwhelmed with happiness and joy when she became a Christian.

After I was released, I was sent back to the Halfway House for the second time. Community Corrections allowed me to minister in churches. Donna invited me to the Freedom

Fellowship support group, and I participated in that weekly get-together. Things were going good.

Then Tina was killed in a car accident in Greeley. She was 19 and had two little girls. That devastated me. I was angry at the Lord—really angry at him.

I started drinking again, got a hot urinalysis, among other violations, and ended up back in prison. When I returned, my heart broke. I cried, not because of landing in prison again, but because I hurt my Lord. I felt like I had betrayed him.

I vowed to myself and to the Lord that I would never do that again. I would serve him with all my heart, with all my mind, and with everything I had. I know the Lord forgave me, and he saw me through the rest of my time in prison.

I miss the closeness I had with God in prison. Prison was my spiritual birthplace; it formed me, gave me my foundation for life. Something beautiful happened to me there.

I also miss the closeness I had with other believers. I remember a man we called "Blue." He was a big, African-American gentleman with arms the size of my waist. Blue was huge, almost seven feet tall.

Although he was a Christian, he was intimidating because he was so large; yet, he and I shared some intimate moments together. We just shared so much, even though my heritage is Hispanic. We never asked each other what our crimes were, because that didn't matter.

One day, however, he cried and told me he murdered his family. He was carrying that terrible burden around. I believe God delivered Blue when he cried and let it all out.

It wasn't about color or about race. It was about a man called Jesus and the fact he died for all of us. I knew God had forgiven Blue, even though some people couldn't forgive him for what he did. I miss that kind of closeness.

The first day I was out of prison, someone gave me a guitar. I began to minister and share the songs I wrote in prison, something like 27 songs. I've been ministering ever since with a band I formed called "Heaven Bound." If God opens a door, Heaven Bound goes in and shares the Gospel. All of our instruments have come from the Lord. God has also blessed us with an awesome sound system and a trailer to transport our equipment to concert locations.

My wife, Priscilla, is a prayer warrior who has intimacy with the Lord, and who stuck with me through all my ups and downs. She could have left me a long time ago, but she kept praying for me. Thanks to her prayers, God did a lot of healing and cleansing and shaping to prepare me for life and ministry on the outside. Priscilla also provided me with three stepsons—James, Darron and Jeremy, who bring much joy to my life.

I haven't had a drink or done drugs since I was released in 1996. God has given me the strength to endure and to stay focused. I thank him for that. Before I gave my life totally to him, I had desires and thoughts and urges, but I can truly say I no longer have a desire to smoke a cigarette, to drink a beer, or to do drugs. God has taken that away from me. If you stay focused and continue to seek him, eventually it will happen.

I think the best testimonies are those of men and women who've been serving the Lord since they were young, who never had to go to prison or go through what I did. On the other hand, some of the strongest ministers and evangelists come out of prison. It goes to show you what God can do, how he can turn evil to good and make it even more powerful.

Jesus' glory seems to rain down in prison. We were seeking him and praising him and giving him thanks all day long. And he rained down his glory. It's a beautiful thing, but a person doesn't have to go to prison to find God.

The best advice I can give inmates and ex-inmates is to stay focused on the Lord, to get involved in a church and in helping others, to give back to the community. Stay in the Word and in prayer. Christian disciplines are essential to the Christian walk—not just for somebody coming out of prison, but for all of us.

It's important to share our testimonies, to talk about how God has changed us. You feel better when you share your story with others and they get something out of it. I believe telling our stories is part of the healing process and part of giving back to the community. It's a great thing to tell others what God has done in our lives.

Chapter 11

Walking in the Spirit
Chaplain Donna Roth, Founder and Director

God directed me to use a unique counseling method, one the prisoners seem to appreciate. The night before I'm scheduled to meet with an inmate, I ask the Lord to give me Scriptures for that person. The verses start "lifting" off the page, or "jumping out at me," as they say.

I don't necessarily read those Scriptures. I just write down the references. When the inmates read them, their mouths drop open, and they say, "Lady, you must be reading my mail." It means a lot to them to have Scriptures personalized for them by God.

I once had a counseling session with a guy who was bragging around the jail that he was a minister. He even preached to the inmates. One day, he put in a request to see me. When God gave me that man's Scriptures, they were all about adultery and stealing. I said, "Lord, I can't give him these verses."

But God told me the man would repent and be set free. It took everything I had to hand him those passages. Sweat was running down my face. He just sat there staring at me, not saying a word. I could hardly breathe.

Finally, he spoke. "I just want to say," he said, "you are the first pastor I've talked with who told me the truth." He prayed right then and repented. I saw a new humility in him to receive God's Word and let it change his life. Every Christian needs to walk the walk, not just talk the talk.

During our prison seminars, I often share stories of what walking in the Spirit means in my life. The stories draw the inmates in. They love hearing how God works. First, I talk about passages in Acts and Corinthians that tell us God will reveal mysteries to us in the Spirit we would never think of in our natural mind. Then I tell them about the time I lost a contact lens and couldn't find it. I searched and searched. Then I remembered that God said in the Bible he would reveal mysteries to us. So I went into my bedroom and started praying in tongues.

And God spoke to me—not audibly, but he told me to get up, walk down the hall, and step into the living room. He told me to get down on my knees and shove my right hand under the couch.

I thought, *Nobody is home, so I can do that without embarrassment.* I stood up, walked down the hall, got on my knees, and slid my right hand under the couch. When I pulled it out, the contact was on the end of my finger.

I also tell them about a supernatural experience that happened shortly after God called me to prison ministry. I was staying the night at my mother's house when, once again, the Lord awakened me. This time, he told me to go into the bathroom.

I was really tired, so it took me awhile to respond. Finally, out of obedience, I crawled out of bed and stumbled into the bathroom, where I said, "Lord, I don't know why you have me in here." And I started praying in tongues.

Suddenly, I heard a big "whish," and a wind came through the bathroom with such force it picked up the rug from the floor and blew it across the room into the hallway.

I gasped in fear, but the Lord said, "Don't be frightened. That was my anointing on your life." And my fear disappeared.

Hearing the commotion, my mother came running in. "What is that rug doing in the hallway."

I said, "You won't believe this, but a wind just came through the bathroom and blew the rug from here to there."

She turned white and ran out the front door but returned immediately. "Donna," she said, "there's not even a breeze outside." I later learned from a pastor that I had experienced the wind of the Holy Spirit.

The story the inmates like the best is the K-Mart story. Several years ago, I had bronchitis. After my doctor examined me, he said, "You have pneumonia, Donna. You've got to get some penicillin."

I thought, *I don't have any money. I'll just have to wait.*

On my way home, I heard a voice say, "Donna, go to K-Mart." I looked around in the car, though I knew it was the Lord speaking.

I said, "Lord, I don't have any money." I had no cash, and I don't carry a debit card or a credit card. There was no way I could get that medicine.

I kept on driving. Again, he said, "Donna, go to K-Mart."

I thought, *I'll just go to Steele's in two weeks, when I get paid. It'll be cheaper there.* And I kept on driving.

I was almost to K-Mart when I heard the voice again. This time it was more demanding, "Donna! Go to K-Mart!"

I released the steering wheel and raised both hands up in the air. "Okay, okay. But I'm going to look like such a fool. I have no money, no charge cards." The Bible says faith without works is dead, so I pulled into K-Mart and went inside. The pharmacist was at the counter.

I gave her the prescription and asked, "How long will this take to fill?"

She said, "About 20 minutes."

So I wandered around the store for a while. Finally, I went back to the counter. I was about to ask the sales girl how much the prescription was, having no idea how I was going to pay for it, when another pharmacist, a man who attended my church, walked up behind her.

He looked over her shoulder, saw me and exclaimed, "Donna Roth, what are you doing here?"

I said, "I just came in to get this penicillin," too embarrassed to tell them I didn't have any money.

He looked at the girl and asked, "How much is Donna's prescription?"

"It's $9.99," she answered. "Why?"

"I've got a coupon for $10. Give Donna her medicine free."

As I walked out with my prescription, I heard the Lord say, "See, I'll always take care of you!"

Inmates also like my Subaru story. Several years ago, I drove an old Honda that kept breaking down. Every time I turned a corner, the engine died. I had to keep taking it in to get fixed.

Eventually, my mechanic said, "Donna, I'm not fixing this car again. The part it needs costs way more than the car is worth. You're going to have to pray for another car."

I responded, "Philippians 4:19 says God will supply all my needs."

On the way home, I prayed, "Lord, you see I need a car here. Nobody's going to fix it for me." And I kept driving it.

A few days later, there was a message on my answering machine with a man's voice saying I was supposed to call an 800 number. I thought he was a bill collector or a salesman, so I did not intend to return the call, but I heard the Lord say, "Call that number."

The person who answered said it was a bank in Boston, Massachusetts. "I know why you were called," he said. "We have a department in our bank where people build up savings accounts and then use the money to help others who are in need. Evidently one of those people learned you have a need."

I said, "I don't know anybody in Boston. I've never even been to the East Coast."

"Well, somebody here knows you."

"No, I don't think so."

"We need to send you this money," he insisted.

"Well, Okay."

The man wanted to make sure he had my address right, so I gave him my current address. In my mind, I figured the amount would be around $200 and thought, *That will be my faith seed money for my new car.*

And I forgot about it. About two weeks later, however, the money came in the mail in the form of a check for $5000 labeled "For a car for Donna Roth."

I thanked the Lord and asked, "What kind of car do you want me to buy?"

He replied, "A Subaru."

I thought, "That's a great car for me. It's good on ice and snow, and I'm not."

My pastor was thrilled with my news. He was always having to rescue me when my car broke down. He said, "Let's go look at Subarus." I didn't see anything I liked at first, so we just kept checking around.

One night when I was asleep, God spoke to me again. He gave me one word—*Legacy*. I had no idea what he was talking about. To me, a legacy was an inheritance left when someone died.

I called my pastor again. "This crazy thing happened," I told him. "God gave me one word when I was sound asleep. He said, 'Legacy.'"

Pastor Dave started laughing. He told me the Legacy is the top-of-the-line Subaru model, the Cadillac of Subarus.

"You're kidding!"

He chuckled, "Yeah, God wants you have a Subaru Legacy." So we started looking at Legacy cars, which started at around $12,000 at that time. I only had $5,000, and the Lord told me I couldn't spend any more than that or make payments.

One day when I was checking my phone messages, I heard a man's voice say, "You don't know me, but I'm a Christian, and I own a car lot in Loveland. Some pastor came in and said, 'There's a lady in Fort Collins who has a prison ministry. She really needs a good car.'"

When I returned the call, the dealer said, "I just wanted to let you know I had a car come in today that I'd like you to look at."

I called Pastor Dave, and we drove to Loveland together. Of course, the car was a Subaru Legacy. It was a one-owner car, a really nice car. The dealer said we could take it to my mechanic to have it checked out.

When we took it in, the mechanic said, "This is a great car. How much do they want? $10,000?"

I said, "The dealer wants $6,900."

The mechanic was amazed.

"But," I added, "when I told him that I only have $5000 and the Lord told me that's all I can spend, the dealer said, 'In that case, I'm going to sell it to you for $5000.'"

The mechanic actually fell over when I told him the price. "That's a miracle!" he exclaimed as we helped him up.

Then I told him I didn't even have to pay the $5,000. Someone else had already sent the money for the car.

I tell prisoners my stories to build their faith in God. Zechariah 4:6 reads, "'Not by might nor by power, but by my Spirit,' says the Lord Almighty." We all need to learn to live by the Spirit, to realize we must depend on God for everything instead of depending on ourselves. I want people to hear God's voice and walk in his freedom and power.

Chapter 12

Growing Up
Brad, Ex-Inmate

Donna Roth and I worked together at a couple of different companies in the late '80s. I didn't understand the entire plan of my friendship with her until the early '90s, when I lost my marriage, my family and my job. By that point in my life, I'd already experienced a great deal of emotional pain and hurt due to the deaths of my brother in a 1966 motorcycle accident, my sister in a 1972 car accident, and my mother, who killed herself in 1984.

I'd stuffed the earlier losses deep inside and hadn't dealt with any of them. Now, I had new issues to deal with. Everything seemed to come tumbling down on top of me. Donna was there for me, as much as I would let her be, during my crisis time.

My whole life was a mess, yet I tried to carry on like everything was fine. Then I started making some unwise financial decisions. Actually, they were more than unwise decisions. I broke the law by writing bad checks.

I think I just decided to not be responsible any more. I was going through major monetary and work-related challenges as well as the divorce. One day, I mentally threw up my hands and said to myself, "Oh, what the heck? One or two bad checks won't hurt."

Well, I wrote more than one or two bad checks, and every one of them caught up with me. I was sentenced to six months at the Larimer County Detention Center. Afterwards I went into the Community Corrections program, but I wrote some more bad checks and was sent to prison for seven months.

When I got out, I knew God wanted me to make restitution, so I went to the businesses I'd issued the checks to, repaid the money, and asked for forgiveness. The business owners and managers were kind and receptive. It was a humbling, cleansing experience.

My growing up has been a process. About four years ago, I committed check fraud again and was sent back through Community Corrections. I guess I had to run into a brick wall a couple of times to get the message.

Before my world fell apart, I was a responsible person. I could maintain a checkbook. I could pay my bills. I could work and be trustworthy—and I was. I just reached a point in my life where everything was piling up on me, and I had no way to deal with it. Irresponsible behavior was my outlet, my way of crying out in the wilderness of life. It was not fun, believe me. I knew my lifestyle was wrong, but I continued to do it anyway.

I've lived in Fort Collins for 20 years and know a lot of people. Because of my incarcerations, I lost several friends, but many stayed beside me. I thank God for them. Donna is at the top of the list.

The second time I was sent to the detention center, I didn't want Donna to see me. I just absolutely did not want her to see me in there. But one day as I was walking down a hallway on my way to play basketball, here she came around the corner. It was an incredibly embarrassing moment, yet I saw the depth of Donna's love and compassion in that encounter. She did not judge me. She did not chastise me. She just let me know she cared.

Ginny and Shirley, both of them Freedom Fellowship volunteers, have also been wonderful friends. I was 32-years old when my mother took her life and did not comprehend how deeply her suicide hurt me as a man. I didn't realize how much I missed my mother and how much pain I had inside. God brought Donna and Shirley and Ginny into my life. He knew I needed godly women who would love and understand me through all the pain.

I became a Christian in the early '90s through a unique set of circumstances related to a guy named Art Fowler. I kept seeing him at a certain restaurant in Fort Collins and wondered what he did for a living, because he was always meeting people there. I couldn't help noticing Art. He's an extremely large man, at least 6 feet 7 inches tall.

One day I asked about his occupation. He said he had a radio and television ministry and met with people to talk to them about the Lord. For some time, God had been working in me, and suddenly I found myself spilling my heart out to Art. I told him all my problems then said, "You know, Art, God brought you into my life for a reason. He knew I needed you."

I met with Art a couple more times before he invited me to his home for dinner with him and his wife. After we ate, I said, "Bring Jesus into my life, Art." And he did. God's presence brought peace and forgiveness.

Although I enjoyed my newfound relationship with God, I still held my pain from the past inside. I'd been the one driving the motorcycle, and my brother was the passenger when we had the accident that killed him. I was 14-years old at the time. Six years later, my sister was killed.

I couldn't process either death. I just stopped up all the pain inside my heart instead of dealing with it. My parents didn't talk about the accidents or about my siblings. I knew my mom and my dad were struggling, but we never talked about our mutual, incredible losses. As far as I remember, none of us received counseling regarding what we'd gone through.

My parents didn't blame me for the motorcycle accident, but I blamed myself. My mom and dad loved me and supported me the best they knew how. Despite their loving attitude, I carried a lot of guilt around for years.

After I graduated from college, I moved to Topeka, Kansas, to sell real estate. One evening while living there, I drove to Washburn University in Topeka to use the law library. I wanted to research the insurance lawsuit related to the accident that killed my brother. I was surprised to learn the suit eventually went before the Kansas Supreme Court.

As I read the review of the court case, I was blown away. My parents had never told me what actually happened. Because I was knocked unconscious by the impact, I remembered none of the details of the collision. The account in the law book said the other driver caused the accident. He caused my brother's death, not me.

The guy was a man with a severe drinking problem who'd been putting up alfalfa hay on my parents' ranch the summer of the accident. I ran into him a couple years after that night in the law library. He broke down and cried and told me how sorry he was. He also told me he accepted Christ as his Savior after the accident and had never touched another drop of alcohol.

I was not a Christian at that time. In fact, I was as far away from Jesus as the east is from the west. Yet, God was beginning his work in me even then, saying, "I've got a plan for you. I'm going to take you from where you are to where I want you to be." Looking back, I can see how God has been working all along in my life.

Having my eyes opened by what I read in the law library was the beginning of my healing process. Later, becoming a Christian purged the guilt from my soul, but I had to learn to receive God's forgiveness and forgive myself.

Some people think emotional healing is immediate, but it often takes time. My heart and my mind had to change in order to release the guilt and view life from a healthy perspective. That's not usually something that happens overnight. For me, change has been a step-by-step process of letting go of the past and its pain and moving forward in God's love.

I've gone through counseling, but my one-on-one relationship with God is what changed my heart. He's still not done with me. I have to be constantly reminded I can do nothing good apart from him.

My healing and maturity has been a process of moving beyond where I've been. I've also had to learn that it's a daily journey. I can't just follow God for a little while, then say, "Okay, God, I'll see you when I need you again."

For years, I wondered where God was during my incarceration. Then one night I read Isaiah 59:2, where it says our sins separate us from God. That verse was a great big wake-up call to me. I have to get on my knees before him every day. That's what keeps me on the right track.

Chapter 13

A Commitment to be Real
Pastor Dave, Board of Directors

When my father-in-law retired from the pastorate, Donna Roth invited him to join her in jail ministry at the Larimer County Detention Center. A few years later, after I moved to Fort Collins to pastor a church, both Donna and my father-in-law encouraged me to go to the jail with them.

I was hesitant and did not respond right away. I hadn't had any experience with jail ministry and did not know whether I would like it, or whether the inmates would like me. I didn't know if that was what God wanted me to do or not. But, through consistent pressure from Donna and my father-in-law, I eventually agreed to participate in a service.

To my surprise, I experienced instantaneous rapport with the inmates. I sensed a great deal of receptivity from them and a great deal of God's love flowing through me for them. My heart was moved with compassion and an interest to minister to the inmates.

After that first visit, I found myself wanting to return again and again. Soon, I was visiting the jail several times a month and participating in the weekend prison seminars several times a year. Then I became a member of the LCDC ministers' board and, eventually, a member of the board of directors for Freedom Fellowship.

I've tried to evaluate the rapport I have with prisoners and finally decided it happens partly because of my personality and partly because of the experiences the Lord has given me. Because the truths of Scripture have been made real in my heart, I have a commitment to be real about my own life, my own failures and weaknesses.

When inmates perceive that those who are ministering to them have something genuine to offer, they are receptive. They are open to volunteers who treat them as peers, as fellow human beings who are fighting the same battles they are and searching for the same solutions. If a person talks down to inmates or has a superior or pitying attitude, his or her words are rejected.

I think rapport also occurs because most of the individuals who attend services in the jail are at the end of their resources and reliance on their own abilities. They're aware of their need for God and are ready to listen in a real, sincere, humble way—often more so than people on the outside. They have time to think about their lives, to read and to pray. They can give concentrated attention to the things of God and what he's trying to say to them.

I'm able to minister to inmates in the jail and other volunteers are able to minister there because of the detention center's governing philosophy. LCDC puts a high priority on the dignity of individual inmates and the importance of treating them with respect. The staff supports volunteer programs that enhance the rehabilitation and educational opportunities they provide to help inmates successfully reintegrate into society.

Administrative officials at the detention center recognize that volunteerism at LCDC reduces tensions and problems among the inmates. I've been told the different ministries within the jail provide a healthy atmosphere and help keep things going smoothly and orderly.

Donna is often called on by the guards and by the counseling staff to meet with people on suicide watch. Inmates experience stress due to loss of freedom, separation from family, financial pressures, and uncertainty about their future. They're oftentimes at risk of killing themselves. When staff members realize that possibility, they put the inmate in a private room and ask Donna to speak with the person.

She's very good at calming the inmates. Sometimes there are tremendous, permanent changes in their demeanors and their attitudes. She says every single person she's been called to minister to on suicide watch has prayed to receive Jesus Christ. Of course, only God knows the inner workings of a soul, but there are often true conversions at those times.

People can be distraught and screaming, but after Donna speaks with them, prays with them, and ministers to them, they come out with smiles on their faces. The guards ask, "What did you do to that person?" Because those amazing changes happen on a regular basis, the guards and the mental health counseling staff regularly ask Donna for assistance.

After a number of years of ministering to inmates, helping with Bible studies, and talking one-on-one with people, Donna was given the title of "volunteer chaplain." Several years later, the administration, in cooperation with the ministers' board, agreed to contract with Freedom Fellowship to provide Donna as the full-time chaplain. One LCDC official told me he believes Donna may be the only paid chaplain in a county jail in the state of Colorado.

The way Donna is paid is unique. She's not employed by the county or paid by taxpayer funds. Instead, the money comes from the Inmate Welfare Fund, which is monitored by the LCDC ministers' board.

The Inmate Welfare Fund is generated through pay-telephone revenues and the commissary where inmates buy hygiene items and food snacks. The fund is used to purchase educational materials, computers, library materials and such, and to pay for contracts with personnel who provide services like haircuts, recreation and, in this case, spiritual ministry.

Everyone who knows Donna recognizes she has a special calling from God for her work. Hundreds and hundreds of inmates have received Christ through her and the ministry of Freedom Fellowship. Freedom Fellowship volunteers hold religious services, Bible studies, discussion groups and support groups within the jail. Volunteers also go in to counsel and encourage on an individual basis.

In addition, the ministry sponsors weekend seminars at state prison facilities and, on occasion, in federal facilities. Weekend seminars normally include teaching, music, worship and testimonies by the volunteers and the inmates. A refreshment break is provided when the facility allows. Occasionally, a prisoner will attend just to get the cookies and end up receiving Christ.

We also set aside a time during each seminar for personal prayer with individual inmates. Many of them battle with depression and discouragement. The seminars lift their spirits. It's not unusual for the inmates to tell us how refreshing and encouraging the weekend is for them.

Our penal system is a ripe harvest field. Jesus said, "Lift up your eyes and look, for the fields are white unto harvest." I don't think that means every single field is "white unto harvest." But there are always fields that are white, ripe and ready to reap. That fact highly motivates me to be involved with the jail and prison ministry. We must spend time reaping those fields.

And the reaping is so rewarding. It's exciting to see those we have ministered to in jail reach a point of stability, maturity and spiritual giftedness where they become responsible, caring people who want to help others, both inside the jails and prisons and outside. All of us at Freedom Fellowship feel privileged to be able to watch God change hearts.

Partnership with the prison ministry has provided tremendous opportunities for members of my congregation to serve God. The jail is a place where those who are new to ministry can share and develop their gifts. It's a place where people who don't have a whole lot of preaching skills can give a testimony of God's grace and have it be an effective tool the Lord uses to transform people's lives.

For those who have musical abilities, jail ministry provides a great opportunity to sing or play an instrument and be used by God to touch inmates ready for a life change. Through Freedom Fellowship, the body of Christ can use its gifts in a meaningful way to build the kingdom of God. Ministering to prisoners has also been used by God in our church to turn our attention away from ourselves to the needs of others, whether physical, spiritual or emotional. People get out of their self-preoccupation and begin to think of others.

As a church, we've become aware of the need for follow-up ministry. When inmates are released, they need support and fellowship. They also need spiritual guidance and Bible teaching. They need a place where they feel acceptance. To help meet those needs, our church and several others in

Fort Collins have hosted the Freedom Fellowship support group for ex-inmates.

We've also seen a need for living quarters where ex-inmates can receive daily fellowship, instruction and support, where a discipleship program is provided on an ongoing basis. We've talked about that need with other prison and jail ministries in northern Colorado as well as other church groups. In recent months, several discipleship houses have opened in our region, for which we praise God. Our desire is to continue to work with area ministries to accomplish great things together for the kingdom of God.

Chapter 14

His Name Was Carlos
Shelly, Inmate's Spouse

One Saturday night when we had nothing to do, my girlfriend said, "Hey, let's call some of the numbers in the singles ads in the paper." It was a game for us, but I left a message on one recording. I liked the sound of the man's voice. Plus, the ad said he loved grandkids, and I have three. He responded with a message, and I left him another message. Finally, we were able to talk by telephone.

He told me his name was Carlos. He also told me he was an alcoholic and a drug addict, and that he really loved God. Before we ended the call, he asked if he could pray with me, which was a surprise and something I wasn't used to, even though I was raised in a Christian home. We talked several times on the phone before we met and became friends. After a year of dating, we were married in May of 1999.

Carlos had been sober for four years, but he was on medication for depression. Though he was bipolar and dependent on the drug for mental health, he stopped taking it and began to drink again. Then he beat me up.

I eventually had to get a restraining order against him. When he broke the restraining order, he was given six months at the Larimer County Detention Center. We didn't see each other or talk for quite some time.

Carlos had met Donna Roth when he was in jail for a previous offense. After he returned to LCDC, I called her and became involved with Freedom Fellowship. I also attended the support group the organization offers for people who are newly released from jail, living in the Halfway House, or on probation, as well as for their families. It helped me to go to the meetings and get to know people who'd "been there."

They knew what I was going through. They knew how degrading the system is. They could tell me what to expect during the process. We prayed together about what each participant was facing that week, whether it was going to court, getting a restraining order, or any other difficult situation.

The support group encouraged me and reminded me that if I would give my problems to God, he would take care of me. It's all a matter of his purposes and timing. We also did some social things together, like picnics and miniature golf.

The group is especially helpful to the people who are in the Halfway House. They go through a lot of stress there because of all the rules and requirements they have to meet. It's a frustrating time for them. The members of the group offer them understanding and encouragement and help them keep focused on their goals.

After Carlos had been in jail for a while, I began to miss him—a lot. I talked with Donna about my feelings. She told me Carlos was doing well, that he was praying, reading his Bible, and going to all the Bible studies and church services at LCDC as well as to AA meetings. It helped me to know she was there to pray with him and counsel and encourage him. I was also glad to know he was spending time with other Christians.

I wrote to Carlos on the fourth of July but waited a couple weeks to mail the letter. I needed to be sure that was what I truly wanted to do. Not too long after, I went before the judge to ask him to modify the restraining order. I didn't know what he was going to say, and I didn't ask if I could visit Carlos in jail.

However, the judge asked me if I wanted to see Carlos. I said "yes," and he said I could visit him. I did a lot of praying before I went to court, because I knew God knew what was going to happen, even though I didn't. I just put it in his hands.

The expression on Carlos' face when he first saw me waiting for him in the visiting area was heartwarming. I was glad to see him. Despite all that had happened, we still loved each other.

We got back together when Carlos was released, and we began to attend the support group and church together. But he started to drink and do drugs and abuse me again, so I had to move to another city to prevent contact between us. Then, on July 21, 2001, Carlos had a heart attack and died.

That was a painful time for me, but I was comforted by the knowledge that Carlos knew and loved God, and that God knew and loved Carlos and took him to be with him in heaven. The support group helped me walk through that difficult period of my life, just like they did while Carlos was incarcerated.

I once attended a Freedom Fellowship seminar at a men's prison. It was a great experience. The men were so receptive. I could tell how much they loved God. I was told they spend a great deal of time studying the Bible and praying together.

Their choir was wonderful and their enthusiasm contagious. Churches in prison are incredibly strong. That weekend opened up a whole new world to me. However, if I were to regularly attend weekend seminars with Freedom Fellowship, I think I would go into women's prisons.

Years ago, I saw a documentary about women prisoners and how they hurt when they can't be with their children and their families. It touched me so much I cried. I talked with Donna and other volunteers about female inmates and decided I'd like to eventually volunteer in women's prisons. That's where my heart is.

Freedom Fellowship does a lot for people on both sides of the bars, but there's much more that could be done. One ex-inmate's wife is talking about researching and coordinating all the assistance available for those in jail or just getting out, like housing, clothing, food, transportation, medical support—anything they might need. I'd like to help her organize that project.

I have done some speaking for Freedom Fellowship at different churches and always enjoy it. People are gracious and interested and have such great questions. It's neat to be a part of something so positive.

Chapter 15

That's Why I Call Him "Father"
David, Ex-Inmate and Former Board Member

I grew up in Rawlins, Wyoming, where I lived with my mom, my two brothers and my four sisters. My stepfather, who tended sheep near Craig, Colorado, was an alcoholic. He didn't give me much attention. My older brother, Daniel, was like a dad to me. My sisters also helped raise me, because my mom was always at work earning money to take care of the seven of us.

Daniel worked for the City of Rawlins. He bought me my first bicycle and took me with him almost everywhere he went. One day, however, when I was eight years old and he was 19, he left me home while he went rabbit hunting with friends. Somehow, he was accidentally shot.

Daniel's friends rushed him into town to the county hospital. My mom was already there with my sister, who was in the process of giving birth to my nephew. Because mom was at the hospital, she was able to be with Daniel when he died. She says he died praying the *Hail, Mary*.

I loved my brother like you wouldn't believe. He was always on my mind, as if he wasn't really dead. I even dreamed about him. At first, I asked God to bring him back. Then I started blaming God because he didn't bring him back. People would tell me God needed Daniel, but that was a bad thing for them to say to me. Although I didn't voice it, I thought, *I need him more than God does.*

That was the beginning of my rebellion against God. I started getting into mischief with my friends. We raided gardens, vandalized property, and other little things like that—at least we thought they were little. Then we started smoking pot and drinking alcohol.

At age 14, I learned the identity of my real dad. That made me very angry. I was mad because I hadn't been able to know him all those years and mad because he never came around. He acted like I didn't exist. He could have at least helped my mom.

As a result, I harbored a lot of anger. I liked to fight. I'm not a very big person, but I used to take on the biggest guys, not caring whether I won or got beat up. I just didn't care.

I drank a lot in high school and sold drugs. I liked art and drafting classes and could have gone to college to be a draftsman. Instead, my heart's desire was to be a guitarist in a rock band. My friends and I planned to move to Colorado after graduation to organize a band.

Only two of us ended up moving. We couldn't find work, so I talked my friend into selling pot with me. Then we added LSD and cocaine to our line. I eventually got a job, but I still sold drugs on the side.

Then I fell in love with a girl named Lona and moved in with her. Lona was not a well person. She had a lung disease, and I knew she didn't feel good. But when I returned home from work one night to find a note on the door from her mom saying Lona had died, I was devastated. All of a sudden, my girlfriend was gone. I blamed God, again.

It seemed like every time I loved someone, he took that person away. I grew leery of loving or caring for anybody but myself. I refused to get close to people, because I was afraid of getting hurt again. I still had an anger problem and was constantly in and out of jail for fighting or driving under the influence.

Shortly after Lona's death, I drove to Cheyenne, Wyoming, to pick up a friend for Thanksgiving dinner. On the way from Cheyenne to Greeley, Colorado, my car rolled off an embankment, and my friend was killed. I went to jail for six months for driving without a license.

I didn't think much about God before that experience. Then I started praying, "Let me out early, God. Get me out of here, and I'll serve you. I'll change my ways."

He got me out, but a month later I was right back to my old habits—getting strung out on cocaine and speed, smoking pot and drinking really bad. I'd come home after work and drink. I'd get up in the middle of the night to drink. I was a bad alcoholic. I was a bad drug addict. I was a bad person.

Then my cousin from Colorado Springs came to visit. We were drinking and partying together, high on drugs and alcohol, and got into a fight that ended when I stabbed him. He'd pinned me down and was choking me, so it was self-defense, but I shouldn't have stabbed him.

I immediately called an ambulance. "Get over here quick!" I said. "I stabbed my cousin. I don't want him to die." I was, of course, arrested. Once again I prayed to God from jail, "Help me get out of here."

My cousin was discharged from the hospital the next day. I was released from jail the next week on a one-year deferred sentence. All I had to do was stay straight for one year, and they would drop the sentence.

I had nowhere to go after I was released, so I lived on the streets. One day I thought, *I should go back to Rawlins, so I'll have a place to stay.* That plan could have worked, if I had told the court. But I had this pride in me that said, *I don't need them. Besides, it wasn't my fault.*

The Colorado authorities soon put a warrant out for my arrest. I ran for two years. It was hard. I was running all the time, always looking over my shoulder, always feeling paranoid about the police.

I got into selling drugs big time, traveling as far as Florida to make drug deals. I constantly carried guns and didn't care if I killed someone. Thank God I never did. And, thank God, I didn't get killed.

The police eventually arrested me in Rawlins. They intended to extradite me to Colorado, but my mom bailed me out, like she always did. However, this time, she said, "One of these days your nine lives are going to run out, David. Someday you're going to get into a jam, and I won't be able to rescue you. Straighten up!"

She and I would have these long talks, and I'd say, "Yeah, yeah, Mom. Right, right."

I bailed out in Rawlins but had to appear in court in Fort Collins within two days. I turned myself in and was sentenced to five years, but I was given another chance. "If you can get a job and find a place to live within a week," I was told, "we'll put you under house arrest."

I remember praying, "God, help me get a job and find a place to live." Sure enough, I found a job and an apartment that day. And I did good for about a month.

But then I thought, *They're not watching me. I can have a few beers. They won't know.*

When I took a breathalyzer test at the reporting center, the officer said, "You've been drinking."

I said, "Yeah, I have."

"Wait here," he said. "We're going to have to arrest you."

I said, "No, you're not!" and took off running, ending up in Arizona with my brother.

Rafael was barely able to take care of himself at that time, so I was a burden to him. There were times when all we had to eat was fruit off the neighbors' trees. It was awful. I thought, *Man, what am I doing here? What am I going to do?* I was at the bottom.

One day when I was driving my brother's car, the police pulled me over. I took off on foot for my brother's house, with police dogs following close behind. As I crawled under his bed, Rafael said, "David, you might as well come out. They're going to get you. I have to tell them you're here." I was mad at him for a long time for turning me in, despite the fact he actually saved my life. The jail provided a place to live and food to eat.

A friend in jail told me about the Lord and asked me to go to Bible studies with him. *I've ruined everything around me,* I thought, *including my relationships with my family and my friends. Maybe I need to try something different.*

My mom never disowned me, but my brothers and sisters were afraid to have me in their homes. I didn't blame them for being scared of me. A person could look at me wrong or say something smart, and I would punch them out. I knew I needed help, so I went to the Bible studies.

After about a month, I was extradited to the Larimer County Detention Center in Fort Collins. I attended everything Freedom Fellowship offered at LCDC. At one of their seminars, I gave my life to the Lord. Then I asked to have a one-on-one with Donna Roth, because I'd heard she gave personalized Scriptures to inmates. Just like I'd been told, Donna brought Bible verses that were obviously just for me and my situation.

Eventually I was sentenced to five years in prison. The week before I was to leave LCDC, Donna said, "I feel the Lord telling me you're going to need to be able to speak in tongues while in prison."

I said, "I don't even know what that is."

She showed me what the Bible has to say about tongues. I said, "Okay." So she prayed with me, and I started speaking in tongues.

"I've never had anybody receive tongues so fast," Donna said. "The Lord was right. He said you were ready for it."

I did need the gift of tongues in prison. There were many times when I was upset and depressed, but I didn't know how to pray, because I was such a new Christian. I would pray in tongues and feel the peace of the Lord come on me and calm me down. I don't know how else I would have survived imprisonment.

I was sent to Behind the Walls, an old territorial prison in Canyon City. Inmates start out there and work their way up to a better prison. If they do badly, they work their way down to a worse prison.

I went through some really hard times at Behind the Walls, because I'd heard the girl I was planning to marry was dating out on the streets. It drove me crazy. One day, I decided to hang myself. But the Lord said, "No! You're not going to do that. Go pray."

I went up to my cell, fell on my knees, and started crying and praying, asking God to help me. As I prayed, I felt the peace of the Lord fall on me like rain and wash me clean.

When I gave my life to Christ, all the drug urges went away. Even so, when I first got to prison, I used downers a couple times to try to dull the pain and loneliness inside. I didn't have anybody. My family was in Wyoming. My girlfriend had deserted me. I was trying to "live on the streets," as they say in prison. A prisoner has to forget the outside world and just do his or her time.

After I took the pain killers, the Lord said, "You either serve me, or you don't serve me. When you're doing drugs, you're not serving me." He showed me a lot in the Bible. In Ezekiel 14, I saw that my girlfriend was an idol in my heart, which made me stumble in my walk with him.

I decided to make my prison experience like a college and take advantage of the opportunity to study the Word of God and form a foundation for the rest of my life. I wanted to be able to teach my future family about God. I studied the Word daily and went to all the Bible studies I could, learning from my brothers in Christ about prayer and fasting and other Christian disciplines. They showed me how to study the Bible. I didn't even know where to find the different books in it or how to use a concordance.

When it was time for advancement to the next prison, I said to a Christian friend, "Let's go pray God will release me from this place." We went out in the yard, sat on the grass and prayed. Then we checked the list of those being moved, but my name wasn't on it. My friend and I prayed again.

About 15 minutes later, the guard called me to his station. "I'm sure your name wasn't on the list before," he said, "but all of a sudden, it popped up on the computer screen." He was freaked out.

My friends all exclaimed, "That's God. That's God!"

At the next prison, everybody told me I wouldn't move up in six months. But six months later, I was advanced again. This time I went to Delta, where they looked at my case and said, "Mr. Martinez, you shouldn't even be in prison."

They saw that the stabbing was self-defense, that I had called the police after the incident, and that I had had a one-year deferred sentence but ended up with five years in prison. "We don't understand why you're in prison," they said.

"I understand why," I told them. "God put me in here because he wanted to get my attention."

About three months before I was to appear before the parole board, I was walking the track outside, when I heard the Lord say, "You're getting out. It's time for you to go home."

I said, "Okay. But Lord, is this really you?" I had a little Bible with me and opened it up to I Corinthians 2:5, where it says we shouldn't put our faith in the wisdom of man, but in the power of God.

"Okay, Lord. I believe, I believe."

I started telling my friends I was getting out soon.

They said, "People with violent crimes don't get out until they do almost all their time."

"Get away from me," I told them. "I don't even want to hear it. The Lord told me I'm getting out, so I'm putting my trust in him."

When it was almost time for me to be released, God told me to go to Harvest Farm, a Christian drug and rehabilitation center near Fort Collins. But I wanted to go home to Rawlins, so I wrestled with God about my decision for a month. He kept telling me to write a letter to Harvest Farm. I kept saying, "No, no, no."

Finally, I said, "Okay, Lord, I'll write the letter."

Just before I went before the parole board, the Lord showed me the Matthew passage, where he says he will give us the words to speak to our governing authorities. So I prayed, "Lord, I'm not even going to think about what I'll say. I'm just going to let you speak."

And that's what I did. I told them the truth. I told them what I was aiming for, and what I was going to do with my life.

The board asked, "If we let you out, where are you going to live?"

"I'm going to Harvest Farm."

"We don't have any paperwork to prove that."

"Let me call Harvest Farm," I said, "to ask if they've accepted me."

So I called the Farm and talked with their chaplain, who said, "We've accepted you. You can come."

When I told the parole board members, they said, "Okay, but you'll have to stay an extra month in prison if you change your parole plan. You can either go home to Rawlins right now or stay here an extra month and then go to Harvest Farm."

I said, "I'll stay in prison, because the Lord wants me to go to the farm. If that's his will, it's going to be good." Even with the extra month, I only served two years of my five-year sentence.

Harvest Farm helped me continue to grow in the Lord and make the transition back into society. God used me to help people with their problems. I prayed with other residents, encouraged them, led several of them to salvation, and even stopped fights. I hadn't expected to be used by God there.

I went to as many Bible studies and support groups as I could at the farm. I also attended a Freedom Fellowship support group in Fort Collins every week. Ginny always picked me up, even when I was the only person going from the farm. It was a blessing, because I needed a break from that environment.

One day, I called Ginny. "Do you know of a place I can rent?" I asked her.

"Not right off hand."

I said, "I'm ready to leave Harvest Farm."

She called me back the next day. "I've got an apartment for rent. You want it?" Ginny managed apartments for a lady and, out of the blue, one of the renters moved out.

"Yes, praise God!" A couple days later, I got a job as a cement finisher. My employer even had someone pick me up because I couldn't drive.

The apartment was in Old Town, next door to bars, which was a battle for me. Satan was always trying to tempt me. I told him, "Get out of here. The man I used to be is dead." I just kept going to support groups and doing everything I was supposed to do while on parole. And I kept asking God to help me.

When I was in prison, I decided I wanted to help young people, so they wouldn't have to go through what I did and wouldn't end up in prison. But I discovered at the farm that it felt good to help other men. I started thinking about becoming a pastor. Right now I'm studying with Pastor Dave to become a licensed minister.

I'm also the outreach director at my church and have started a ministry called Dreams In Christ Ministry to help ex-offenders, homeless people, and drug addicts. Plus, I'm in the process of establishing halfway houses for guys who come out of prison. I know that if God can help me, he can help anybody.

I'd like to provide homes for kids, where we can teach them trades, so they don't have to sell drugs or their bodies to take care of themselves. I want to teach them how to use computers. I'd like to help them purchase their own homes. That's just part of what I think Dreams in Christ is going to do.

Freedom Fellowship played a big part in getting me through my three years of parole. Now I can go back into the prisons and the jails and tell the residents, "If you stick with the Lord, with a support group, and with godly people to guide you, you can make it." But it takes a lot of commitment and hard work.

I thank God for sending me to prison. Not only did I find the Lord through imprisonment, but as a result of seeing the changes in my life, my mom and stepdad gave their lives to the Lord. One of my sisters has become a believer. My nephew, who thought I'd never change, is beginning to seek God.

A few months ago, I prayed for my sister Melina, who had a twisted leg and limped. She said it felt like a flash of fire shot down her back and into her leg when I prayed. God allowed me to watch her leg straighten as he healed it. Now, praise God, Melina walks with no sign of a limp!

In addition to all the other blessings in my life, God has given me a wonderful wife—a beautiful Christian woman named Sandra. She has a daughter, Angela, and I love them both very, very much.

When I was a little boy, I often talked to an invisible somebody as I played alone in the yard with my toys. After I became a Christian, the Lord told me, "The person you were talking to out in the yard was me."

I started crying. "You were *always* my father," I sobbed. "You were *always* there for me." That's why I call him "Father."

Chapter 16

Road to Freedom
Shirley, Volunteer

After my husband died, I moved to Fort Collins to live with one of my sons and his family. I didn't have any friends in town, so I called my church office to ask about joining a small group. The secretary gave me three telephone numbers.

The first person I called told me they didn't have room for any more people in their group. The second person said their group was no longer meeting. And the third person said, "We don't meet in homes. We go to the jail."

I thought, *OK, Lord, that must be where you want me.*

My husband and I had been involved in a jail ministry for six years in North Platte, Nebraska. We also managed a halfway house for several years. Ministering to inmates and ex-inmates was not a new venture for me.

Despite my extensive experience, the volunteer coordinator at the Larimer County Detention Center told me she thought I was too old to work in the jail. I was 67 at the time. She thought the men would con me.

I told her, "I have four sons and 10 grandsons. I don't think so." She agreed and allowed me to go in as a volunteer.

I went with the group on Monday evenings and really enjoyed visiting with the prisoners. Then I heard about a team that went to LCDC on Sunday afternoons and decided to join them. I hadn't been invited, so I guess you could call it "jail crashing," but they didn't seem to mind.

131

I've been involved in almost all aspects of Freedom Fellowship's ministry at the jail. Right now I lead the men's Bible study on Monday afternoons. Sometimes I go in on Tuesday or Thursday for one-on-one sessions. I'm also a part of the ex-inmate support group leadership team. On Fridays, I teach interested inmates the mental health program that helped me overcome mental illness.

The inmates are usually surprised to learn that in the '60s I was a mental patient who attempted suicide three times and that I was in and out of psychiatric hospitals for nine years. One inmate told me, "When I first saw you, Shirley, I thought, *Big deal, what does she know about life?* But after I heard you talk, I thought, *She does that life can be hard.*"

I tell the inmates I was a drug addict and a very bad person. I was a prescription addict. But let me tell you, it's just as much of an addiction as an illegal habit. I drank alcohol along with taking the pills and had the kind of lifestyle that goes with all that.

Because two of our sons were accidentally killed within one year, the doctors gave me pills and gave me pills—and gave me more pills. I even took them *just in case* I might get nervous. I was addicted.

When he finally took the pills away, the doctor said, "If you can't stand it, Shirley, call me. I'll give you something to get you by."

As you might imagine, the withdrawal was horrible. My entire body shook for days. After a week, I called the doctor. He said, "I'm sorry, Shirley, but I'm not going to give you anything." He knew I would be alright, because I'd lasted that long.

After going through addiction and withdrawal, I can tell people, "Hey, I don't care what you've done or what you've been through, God is able." I tell the prisoners I know they've tried with everything that's in them to escape their addictions, because that's what I did. I tried so hard. If I hadn't become a Christian, experienced the baptism of the Holy Spirit, and discovered the "Road to Freedom" mental health program, I'd still be struggling—or dead.

The Lord saved and baptized my psychiatrist in the Holy Spirit. When he told me about his experience, I thought, *I have no idea what he's talking about.* I asked a priest in my mental health group about the baptism of the Holy Spirit. He said he had received the baptism. I asked him to pray for me. God in his mercy saved me, baptized me, delivered me, and made me a new creation. I still get goose bumps when I think about how God works.

He not only healed my mind, he healed my marriage. Glenn and I had been married for 25 years, but our relationship was a total disaster. Glenn had even tried to kill me. God saved both of us, healed both our minds. We had 21 more good years together before he died.

There isn't anything that surprises me. I know what people are going through. And I know what God can do.

The "Road to Freedom" mental health program taught me how to live a balanced life. I teach it at LCDC, because I feel the inmates can use the tools the program offers. The Bible tells us what to do, but how do you do it? That's what the program teaches.

"Road to Freedom" was developed by a psychiatrist and has descriptive, easy-to-remember phrases like "distressing but not dangerous," which helped me when I had nervous symptoms; and "feelings are not facts," which reminds us that our feelings will lie to us and tell us something is a big deal when it's trivial.

The program works because it teaches people how to handle anger and fear. I have been sending the "Road to Freedom" lessons to my two grandsons, who are in prison. One recently sent me a letter. "Grandma," he wrote, "I'm going to go through those lessons again. I have to learn to control my temper."

I know what he means. In the '60s, I was so out of control I ran away, leaving my five children without a mother, even though my oldest son was in bed with the flu. I rode the train 300 miles to the Nebraska Psychiatric Institute in Omaha and told them, "I think there's something wrong with me."

They said, "We don't see anything wrong with you."

I said, "Then maybe I should call my family and tell them where I am."

"You mean nobody knows where you are?"

"No."

They said, "Sit right here," and called Glenn.

Glenn told them, "You've got her, you keep her."

That first NPI hospitalization lasted three months. I returned every year for nine years. They tried every treatment they had, and I took every pill they offered me, which was a bunch. Every time a new drug came out, they gave it to me. I once attempted suicide with an entire bottle of Valium.

But God in his mercy didn't let me die. I wouldn't have gone to heaven if I'd died then, and I've always wondered who was praying. Maybe Jesus himself was interceding for me.

Glenn had also been a mental patient. In 1954, he was charged with "assault with intent to do great bodily harm" to a woman he attacked. I took him to NPI, where he stayed for several months.

After the deaths of our sons, Glenn went to college to get a degree in psychology to try to help both of us. During the course of his training, he discovered that the professionals don't always have the answers.

I had the same experience. One time when I was out on the patio breaking jars to release my anger, as I'd been taught, my young daughter walked out. "Mom," she said, "if you're going to make this kind of mess, you're going to clean it up." The wisdom of my child taught me more than all my therapists and psychiatrists put together.

"Road to Freedom" teaches a person how to deal with anger, not just how to express it. When I started the program, I thought, *I'll do this, but it ain't gonna help. Nothing has helped.* However, when I saw an older lady improve, I thought, *If Jenny can get well, I bet I can too.*

Of course, a person has to practice what they're taught, and they have to try. But they have to know how to try. God led me to this program to help me gain mental balance in my life, and it worked for me.

About a year after I first got involved with Freedom Fellowship, God brought Shanna into my life. After she was released from jail, I was at her doorstep every morning. I took her to community corrections, to do her urine analyses, to talk to her parole officer—whatever she needed. I also took her to church and to the ex-inmate support group.

Shanna and I became great friends. But sometimes I would be talking to Shanna and suddenly realize she was just sitting there staring at me. It made me uncomfortable. Eventually I'd ask, "Shanna, why are you doing that?"

"I'm listening to you," she'd say.

And I'd pray, *Oh, Lord, help me to say the right things to this girl. Don't let me lead her wrong.*

I was with Shanna most of the time when she was first released. We ate lunch together nearly every day. I took her to Wendy's, where she applied for a job as soon as she got out of jail. They hired her, and she worked for them for over a year.

At one point, Shanna had to go back to LCDC for five days. When I went to pick her up, I didn't know what to say to her, so I didn't say anything. I was just sick. But Shanna says that's when she decided, *Okay. It's either all the way for God or nothing.* And that's how she's lived ever since.

Shanna is now married to a very good husband who is a strong Christian. They have a great marriage and are both active in a puppet ministry at their church. They also have a sweet little baby girl.

I'm so thankful to have been with Freedom Fellowship for almost eight years. During these years, I've gained many inmate friends and many volunteer friends. They're some of the neatest people in the world.

What a privilege it is for me to volunteer in the jail. I am so blessed. Like the old hymn says, it's a "joy unspeakable and full of glory" to get to do these things at my age!

Chapter 17

Free on the Inside
Joseph, Inmate

My first encounter with God occurred when I was 15-years old and on the run from a juvenile institution. My girlfriend, Carrie, and I were staying with my cousin in Portland, Oregon. One Sunday, his wife asked us to go to church with her at the Church of the Living Water. All I had in my pocket that morning was 20 cents, but I put it in the offering plate.

After the service, Carrie and I decided to walk home. Two or three blocks from the church, we heard a voice say, "Young man ..."

We turned around. There stood an elderly couple. "Young man," the old man said, holding out a $20 bill, "God told me to give this to you."

I refused it three or four times. Finally, I took the money. Immediately after we gave our last 20 cents to God, he gave it back to us a hundredfold. That experience made an impression, although I still didn't include God in my life.

I had another encounter with God when I was 19-years old. Carrie and I were driving across Texas with our toddler son and our baby daughter. Things weren't going too good for us. I had just met my birth mom for the first time, Carrie and I had had an argument that ended in violence, and we had no money. On top of all that, at two o'clock in the morning, in the middle of the Texas panhandle, our car broke down.

I jerked open the car door, jumped out, and yelled at the sky, "God, why? Why!" I was extremely angry, but I also had tears in my eyes. As I stared into the night, I saw headlights coming from the opposite direction.

The car passed us then turned around and drove toward us. I figured it was a patrolman, but when the car pulled up, an elderly Hispanic man got out. "How are you doing?" he asked.

I explained our situation to him. He said, "Get your wife and children and come with me."

He took us to a little church in a nearby small town. "I go to church here," he told us, leading us to a room in the basement containing three beds and a crib. That night we each slept in a bed of our own and had a good rest. Early the next morning, the man returned with his wife.

"Let's go take a look at your car," he said, as we got into his vehicle.

"I know what's wrong with it," I said. "My alternator is out."

He immediately hit the brake pedal, turned a corner, and stopped in front of an old shed. We stepped inside. There on a dusty shelf sat an alternator. "Will this one fit?" he asked.

I told him I thought it would, and we drove out to my car to install it.

Meanwhile, Carrie and the kids were shopping with the man's wife and another woman. They bought groceries and diapers for us. As we drove away, those kind people called, "We love you. Be careful. God bless you."

Here I was, yelling at God, angry at him for the way I had caused problems in my life and everyone's lives around me, yet he still took care of me.

Despite God's love and provision, I continued to ignore him. Eventually, I lost my wife and my family. I also ended up in prison with theft and assault convictions due to alcohol and drug abuse.

One day, while I was sitting in the prison chow hall looking at the men around me, their faces all went blank. That caught my attention, to say the least. I hurried back to my cell to look at my reflection in the mirror and was shocked to see that I had the same blank look on my own face. It was like I was dead, like we were all dead.

I fell to my knees, begging God to make me a better man. "God," I said, "show me what I'm supposed to do here."

I grabbed the Bible off my bookshelf and opened it, landing on Joshua 1:8, "This book of the law shall not depart from your mouth …"

As I got up off my knees, I was sobbing. I remember hearing a guy a couple of cells down the row ask, "What's the matter?" I didn't answer him.

I'd never read that Bible before. It was only there for looks, just another book on my shelf. I believe God reached down to let me know I was his, to let me know he cared. He hadn't abandoned me, but had allowed me to go astray in my life to learn I have nothing without him.

After the chow hall experience, my life began to change. I dealt with people and with my emotions differently. I no longer tried to fit into the prison environment. I went to church and read my Bible. When Christians talked about the things of God, it made sense. I started going to all the prison services, not just one every couple of months.

One day a volunteer named Jim came to one of the prison Bible studies. Afterwards, the two of us went into a private room, where I told him my story about the blank faces.

He said, "Sounds like Christ revealed himself to you. It's time to 'put up or shut up.'"

"Would you help me?" I asked.

I had heard about accepting Jesus, but I didn't know how to do it. As we prayed together, I asked Christ to come into my heart to be the Lord of my life. At that moment, I was cleansed, and the void in my life was filled.

There were times in my past when I had lots of money and plenty of alcohol, drugs and women, but I was still empty. With God in my life, I wasn't empty any more, even though I had very few material possessions.

As my prison sentence drew to a close, I realized I didn't have a place to go when I was released. I prayed about my situation for several months. Although I had no friends or relatives in Fort Collins, God said, "Joseph, go to Fort Collins when you get out of prison."

I asked for a reason but did not get an immediate answer. Then, not long before my release, Freedom Fellowship showed up at a Sunday service. After the service, I spoke with the volunteers.

"I enjoyed the service," I told them, "and would like to know where you attend church. I need a good church to go to when I get out. I need fellowship and reinforcement in my life." They gave me the phone numbers for Freedom Fellowship and Northgate Church on the Rock in Fort Collins.

A couple days later, the reintegration specialist at the prison said to me, "Joseph, I couldn't find you a place to stay in Denver (where I was from), but there's a place in Fort Collins where we can get you a room for one week."

It was like God telling me, "Yes, Joe, this is really where you are supposed to go."

Two weeks later, I walked from the hotel in Fort Collins over to Northgate Church on the Rock and introduced myself to Pastor Dave. We talked for quite a while. He asked me some serious questions about my relationship with God. I answered them to the best of my ability.

I also called the Freedom Fellowship phone number and ended up being surrounded by a whole group of people who love me and who forget my past and let me go forward. They are always supportive. If I have questions or need understanding or wisdom, I can go to Donna or Pastor Dave. If I need someone to listen to me ramble, I can call Ginny. If I want fellowship or encouragement, I can go to a Freedom Fellowship Bible study.

With Freedom Fellowship, God is first and foremost. Their sole purpose, their mission, is to teach people that God loves them. That was apparent to me from the moment I walked into my first Freedom Fellowship service.

I'm incarcerated at Larimer County Detention Center at the moment, because I got upset about a situation with my kids, started drinking, and was eventually arrested for driving drunk. When I went to court, Donna was there.

She said, "I'm waiting to see another person who was supposed to go to court today, but I checked the docket, and they're not even on the list." Then she added, "You know, Joseph, I'm here for a reason. God is going to give you another chance."

I said, "Yes, Ma'am, I believe that."

I could have gone back to prison or been put on parole, but I was sent to LCDC. God wanted me to wake up and realize I need him. I can't put anybody else first—myself, my parents, or my children. God used the government to incarcerate me for a little while to get my head straight.

The day I get out of LCDC, I'll be knocking at Northgate Church on the Rock and Freedom Fellowship's support group. I need Christian fellowship—not people talking about drugs, booze and illicit sex. I need God, Christian love, positive things—fun without drugs. I want to get up early to see the sunrise. I want to take my grandson to the park to feed the ducks.

I view life differently now. I'm not the man I was, nor will I ever go back that way again. I'm not perfect. I still make mistakes, get angry, have wrong emotions. But instead of dealing with things the way I used to, I go to God. He helps me understand situations before I act on them.

When I open the Word of God, it's not just writing on a page. It's his Word teaching me how to live. The more I put his words into my heart, and the more his teaching is impressed into my mind, the less likely I am to repeat my mistakes.

"Put up or shut up" keeps ringing in my ears. Things I did in my past have affected my children, my parents, and my peers. I want my words to benefit my children, and my actions to say that God is real. He changes lives. He takes the detestable and makes it acceptable.

I know God loves me. I know I'm forgiven. The truth I have in my life will not alter, will never change. The only mistake I can make now is to not rely on God. I'm incarcerated because I tried to do it my way without asking God for counsel.

My priorities are different than they used to be. The books I read, the television programs I watch, and the music I listen to are all different. Sometimes when I'm watching TV with a group of men, I have to get up and leave because I know what I'm viewing is wrong. Before, I would have just sat there. My life is totally different. The other inmates respect that.

There was a time in my life when they would have respected me ... or else. But now, they respect me for who I am and what I believe in. I don't hide my beliefs, but I don't beat people over the head with my Bible either. Guys often come up and ask me questions about Scripture. That makes me feel good.

When the men in here complain, I tell them there are people on the outside who are deaf, dumb, blind or starving. We even have carpet on the floor. I see blessings where I used to see oppression by the establishment. The establishment didn't put me here. I put me here.

But I'm free on the inside. I have clothing, food, friendship and fellowship. There are more opportunities to be blessed in this jail than I ever experienced on the streets. I'm alive and healthy and growing stronger every day. God is good.

When I get up in the morning, the first thing I do is put on my socks, brush my teeth, and grab my "Daily Bread." I read it and pray before I do anything else. A couple of mornings, I didn't have my time with God. Those days were the pits. Everything that could possibly go wrong or irritate me did just that.

I said, "Please God, I'm about to snap. Would you help me?"

Then the thought came to me, *Pray when you get up.*

That's what I do now, even if I only have five or ten minutes. No matter what happens, I can deal with the situation. Sometimes I just pray, "Lord, thank you that I'm alive. Please help me not to be a knucklehead today."

The encouragement Freedom Fellowship volunteers give me has helped me go through with some of the things God wants me to do. He's changing my life and allowing me to lead others to him.

There's a double portion of the Spirit behind bars. More and more people are finding God in prison. I believe with all my heart that thousands, maybe millions, of once-incarcerated people will walk the streets of heaven someday. I'll be one of them.

Chapter 18

You Are My Provider
Chaplain Donna Roth, Founder and Director

The first time I held my beautiful newborn granddaughter, the Lord spoke to me. "Your grandchild just came from her mother's womb," he said. "She can do nothing for herself. She completely depends on her mommy for *everything*. That's how my people should depend on me."

Three years ago, I discovered in Malachi 3:8-12 that tithing is an important aspect of trusting God and receiving his blessings. Those verses tell us that we rob God when we don't tithe, which is giving 10 percent of our earnings back to him.

God also tells us in Malachi 3 to test him to see if he will open the windows of heaven and bless us when we give our tithes. After I read that passage, I decided to do just that. So I went to King Soopers, where I buy money orders to pay my bills. The first money order I requested was for my tithe. Then I paid the other bills.

When I was done, there was no money left for food. I told the Lord, "I'll just go on home."

Before I even got to the door of the store, a man yelled out, "Donna Roth!" and ran over to me.

"Donna," he said, "do you remember me?"

"Yes, I do."

He smiled. "I was in jail three years ago. You led me to the Lord, baptized me in water, and prayed with me for the baptism of the Holy Spirit. Now I'm married to a Christian woman, and we are following the Lord together. Plus, we have a new baby."

"Praise the Lord!" I exclaimed.

"I have my own business," he added, "and it's doing great. The Lord told me to give you this money."

I thanked him, gave him a hug, and he left the store. I looked at the check. It was written for the exact amount of my tithe. As I stood there praising God, I heard him say to me, "There's your money for your food." God is so good!

Later on, while I was eating cake at a wedding reception, I suddenly thought, *I am totally out of money. I don't know how I'm going to make it for the next two weeks.*

Then I thought, *I know, I'll just borrow from my mom.*

But the Lord immediately said to me, "I hate borrowing!"

"Okay, Lord," I said. "I won't borrow. I'll just wait on you."

Just then two ladies I hadn't seen for many years walked up to me. One of them said, "Donna, my cousin was at the end of the cake line and I was at the beginning of the line, when the Lord spoke to both of us and told us to each give you $100." They handed me the money, and I cried, knowing God was once again providing, because he loves me and because I was obedient.

After a prison volunteer shared his ministry needs at church one Sunday, we were given an opportunity to contribute to his work. I had just paid my tithe and my bills and only had $20 left in my purse to cover my needs for the next two weeks.

The Lord said, "Donna, put your last $20 in the offering bucket. I want to bless my servant."

I said, "But, Lord, this is all I have."

The Lord again said, "Put the $20 in the bucket."

I finally surrendered and dropped the bill in the offering bucket, thinking, *I don't have a cent of money now, Lord, but that's okay, because you are my Provider.* Then I forgot about the money and listened to a wonderful message by the pastor.

Just as I was leaving the sanctuary, a woman called out, "Donna Roth, wait! I have something for you." She walked over and handed me a folded check. I thanked her for her kindness and put the check in my Bible.

As I slid the check between the pages, I could see a "2" and a "0." *Praise the Lord!* I thought. *I haven't even left the church building and I've received back my $20.*

When I got home, I took the check out of my Bible to put into my wallet. As I opened it, I was shocked to see that the amount was not $20, but $200. I heard the Lord say, "See, I gave you back tenfold for obeying me."

One Sunday morning, I spoke at a church about jail and prison ministry. The pastor asked me to return that evening to teach about the baptism of the Holy Spirit. So I did, and many received the baptism that night. When I was leaving, the pastor said, "Here's a check for your ministry. We also took an offering for your personal needs."

I expected maybe $50, but when I opened the personal check, it was written for $400 and labeled "a gift for Donna Roth." What a blessing! God again provided.

Recently, I was visiting with a pastor about jail and prison ministry. As we talked, I heard the Lord's voice say, *Tell him about your washer.* So I asked the pastor if he could put a note in the Sunday bulletin notifying his congregation that I needed a new washer, because mine was broken beyond repair.

The pastor looked at me for a moment before saying, "Go buy a new washer."

"I don't have any money."

"I know you don't, but we do. Go get a new washer. We'll pay for it." That very week, a brand new washer was delivered to my home.

Before I left for Africa, I sat down in church next to a lady who was wearing the most beautiful blue dress. It was a vibrant blue, and the design looked African to me. I said to myself, *I would love to take that dress to Africa.* I said to the lady, "What a beautiful dress! That would be perfect for my trip to Africa."

I was hoping she would tell me where she got it, but she just said, "Thank you."

After the service, I walked out to my car with my mother. Suddenly, I heard the Lord say, "Donna, go to K-Mart."

I looked at my mom and said, "We're going to K-Mart."

When we got there, I looked through the dresses but didn't see any blue ones. Then I heard the Lord say, "Go to the clearance rack in the back of the store." I didn't even know K-Mart had a clearance rack.

But I went to the back and, sure enough, there stood a huge clearance rack full of summer wear. I started at one end of the rack. When I got to the middle, I gasped. There was the dress the woman at church had worn, in the same bright blue color. I thought, *Surely it's not my size.* (Oh, me of little faith!)

But when I turned the tag over, it was my exact size—and it was the only dress on the rack of that style and color.

I said, "Thank you, Jesus!" and proceeded to the checkout counter. What a miracle! God gives us the desires of our hearts. I no longer have that dress because I gave all the clothing in my suitcase to the poor people in Africa. What a joy it is to obey God's voice.

I tell these stories to the inmates to demonstrate how God has blessed me when I've been obedient to him. I can say without hesitation, "You'll be blessed when you tithe. Obey the Lord."

Chapter 19

Just Walking with God
Vanita, Board of Directors

I'd been going to Northgate Church on the Rock for only five or six months, when Pastor Dave announced that his father-in-law and Donna Roth were inviting others to join them in their jail ministry. He asked those who were interested to raise their hands. I raised mine, went through the background check, and soon attended my first church service in jail.

There were six or seven of us from Church on the Rock who participated that first Sunday afternoon. I came away with such a blessing. It seemed like the men and women were so hungry to hear the Word of God. We went every week for two years. Then other churches started rotating Sundays with us.

That was more than nine years ago. Jail ministry had never crossed my mind before that time. I believed that people who were imprisoned deserved to be there. They didn't treat other people right, so why should they be treated good?

Now I look at prisoners differently. Yes, they need to be incarcerated, but they also need to be treated kindly and to have Jesus Christ as their Savior and Lord.

I went with a spirit of curiosity and was truly amazed at what I learned. The inmates I met were just sad, lost people. A lot of the bad things they did were a result of the way they were raised. Some of them grew up in really bad homes.

Others were given everything money could buy but weren't offered love or time with their parents. Some were never taught the difference between right and wrong. Now they were hungry to learn about God and hungry for the love he offers.

They could relate to Jesus, who didn't have an easy life, and to Paul, who spent a lot of time in prison. A person might wonder what good Paul did in prison. I once heard Pastor Dave tell a group of inmates: "The Apostle Paul wrote entire books of the Bible while he was incarcerated. You, too, can do great things for God behind bars."

Quite a few people from our church, including myself, also started going to the state prisons with Donna and Freedom Fellowship. I was so impressed with the way the inmates sat on the edges of their seats, soaking up every word. They were full of questions.

It was a whole different atmosphere than church on the outside. No one whispered or rustled papers or roamed in and out of the room. The prisoners just sat there absorbing every bit of what we had to say.

At the prison seminars, we stress the fact that God loves everyone, no matter what they've done, no matter what crime they've committed. Inmates can ask for forgiveness, invite Jesus into their hearts, and become children of God. We tell them that God cares, and that they can turn to him for every need they have.

Prisoners are fellow human beings who have the same spiritual and emotional needs and feelings as those of us on the outside. When we voluntarily go behind bars, our presence tells the inmates, "We care about you as a person, and we'd like to see you go to heaven."

I've been on the Freedom Fellowship board for several years. It's a great organization. We do a lot with support groups and helping people after they get out of LCDC. Donna is good at finding clothing. When people are released from jail, they often don't have anything except the clothes they were wearing when they were arrested. In the wintertime, they need coats and gloves and other warm clothing.

We arrange for drivers to pick people up at LCDC and drive them to the bus depot. Sometimes, we find agencies that will help an ex-offender buy a bus ticket home. We also pick up individuals who are on probation or at the Halfway House and take them to church or to the support group.

Our ultimate goal is for inmates and ex-inmates to grow in their faith. Even with our support, they often struggle with walking the straight and narrow. If they don't stay in church and in the support group and Bible studies, many of them return to their old ways.

It used to bother me when someone ended up back in jail. I'd be disappointed with that person. Then I realized Christianity is a growing process that God can handle. He's awesome, and he does amazing things in all of our lives.

We need more volunteers to mentor ex-inmates when they are released. It takes time and dedication and a willingness to go the extra mile. But that extra mile can make all the difference in an ex-inmate's life.

Pastor Dave, Donna and I do baptisms at LCDC once a month in the jail bathtub. I don't think we've ever baptized less than eight people, and we once baptized 21. Last month, we had five men and 11 women. I did the baptizing because Donna was sick and Pastor Dave was gone. Before I went, I said, "Lord, I can't do this. I know I can't do it. But you can." And he did.

Freedom Fellowship is a great avenue and opportunity for anyone interested in ministering in jail. It's a wonderful place to reach people for the Lord. Some of the prisoners don't even know what they're looking for. They're just searching, like a man I met a long time ago.

He said to me, "I sure want what you have."

I thought, *What do I have? I'm living in low-rent housing. I don't know where the next meal is coming from. I've got all these kids and not much else, certainly nothing fancy.* I couldn't figure out why he wanted what I had.

I must have had a puzzled look on my face, because he said, "I don't mean money. I mean, you have this shine about you. There's something different about you."

My relationship with the Lord was what he desired for himself. I prayed with him and told him, "It's just walking with God. That's all I can tell you—walk with the Lord. Trust him."

Because I trust God, I call on him all the time. I don't just expect miracles, I rely on them. And that's how we operate at Freedom Fellowship. We rely on God's love and power to work through the volunteers, so he can miraculously change the lives of incarcerated individuals.

Chapter 20

Does She Have Tattoos?

Scott, Donna Roth's Grandson

As long as I can remember, my grandma, Donna Roth, has been working at the jail. It actually seems normal to me to have a grandma who's in prison most of the time. My family likes to tell the story about what I said when I was five-years old. We were all meeting at Pizza Hut to eat. When Grandma walked in the door, I hollered, "Grandma, do you get to eat some pizza before you go to jail?" I've been told people dropped silverware, stopped eating, and turned to stare at her.

But to me, it was and is a natural thing for my grandmother to be in jail. Sometimes I tell my friends she's in jail or going to prison for the weekend.

They say things like: "Wow! What did she do?" "Does she have tattoos?" "Is it cool to have a grandma in prison?" I laugh and tell them she works at the jail.

Grandma started taking me to church when I was just a baby. I was always in the nursery or Sunday school. She even baptized me when I was eight-years old. Sometimes she picked up ex-inmates from the Halfway House to take them to church with us. When I was little, they played with me and bounced me on their knees. I had a lot of fun with them.

When I heard Freedom Fellowship was going to Uganda last summer, I told my grandma, "I want to go to Africa with you."

She said, "There's no McDonald's there, Scott. Uganda is a lot different than America." Still, even though I was a typical teenager, I really wanted to go.

I love music and I play several instruments. So I was thrilled when I was asked to be the drummer for the praise and worship team that was going on the trip. Later, they decided they didn't need me after all.

My grandma said, "You probably don't want to go to Uganda now that they don't need you in the band."

I told her: "I feel called to go to Africa. I'm going to let God use me however he wants."

I ended up playing drums and guitar at the meetings in Uganda, a lot more than I expected. I even got to play guitar with the local band. They told me I "got their beat," which was a real compliment. Their band members were all very good. They each played several instruments, and they were all great singers. They're very talented musicians.

I was also asked to speak to a group of Ugandan kids when we visited a school there. I told them how great my grandma is, that she raised me spiritually, and that I'm glad she did. "If it wasn't for her teaching me about Jesus," I said, "I wouldn't be going to heaven." Then I told them that Jesus died on the cross for them, too.

I also said that though they think we Americans are rich, actually they are the ones who are rich, because they have so much love for one another. People are incredibly nice and caring in Uganda, toward everybody. Well, everybody except prisoners.

I went to only one prison in Uganda. It was a horrible place. The conditions were awful. Seeing the lack of hope on the prisoners' faces was sad. They looked sick and starved and very deprived. Their shirts were ragged and torn. One man was wrapped in a blanket—that was all. Unless the families take care of prisoners, they have no clothing provided for them.

It was hard to be at that prison knowing that those who had more than a year sentence would probably die there. It was depressing. I'm not sure I ever want to go to prison again, even in America. You know terrible conditions exist in the world, but until you see it first-hand, it's not real in your mind.

My grandma wanted me to pray for the prisoners. I said, "I don't know how to pray for them," but I prayed anyway. Lots of inmates came to the Lord at that prison, and we prayed for many others to be healed from sickness.

One guy told me he'd been beaten by the police when he was arrested and that he was still bleeding internally. I could see he'd been roughed up. He also said he had a broken rib. I didn't know the whole story, so I prayed that the right thing would happen to the right people.

The first week we were in Uganda, I became friends with the guys who worked in the hotel where we stayed. They make about 25 cents a month and work almost 24 hours a day. Before we left, I gave them the rest of my spending money, which was less than 20 bucks, but it was like several years' worth of pay for them. That made them really happy, although it was nothing for me to give it to them. They ended up joining our group when we prayed together before we checked out of the hotel.

The hotel rooms left a bit to be desired. Two of the ladies went crazy when they found a huge cockroach in their room. I thought it was cute, but they didn't. They moved to a different room. Then a lizard crawled under their door. They went nuts again. It was great.

I liked the Ugandan food. We ate a lot of goat, beef and chicken, including chicken gizzards at every meal. The breads were excellent, and their fruit was incredible—very good, fresh fruit. I also enjoyed the fried bananas.

I even made friends with our dinner. I named a goat "Billy," and later we ate it. I think we also ate a chicken Pastor Dave received as a gift, because it just disappeared.

Uganda had a few fast food places. We ate one time at a place called "Steers" that was supposed to be like a McDonald's. I got a tiny little hamburger that tasted terrible. But, they had good ice cream and good pizza in Uganda.

One day when we were driving down the road with all the windows open, we stopped at an intersection. Suddenly, people came running toward our van with cooked food on sticks, like chicken on a stake, pork on a stake, and cold pops. They shoved the food through the open windows, right in our faces, yelling, "Buy, buy, buy!"

One of our Ugandan friends laughed and said, "This is what you call a drive-through restaurant in America!" I just bought water. We drank a lot of bottled water there.

Speaking of water, the hotel had cold water for showers; never warm water. The second week, we stayed at a house where we heated up a bucket of water then poured it over ourselves. Only the upper-class homes have actual showers.

When I got back home, I went straight to our bathroom and sat down on the toilet. I didn't even need to use it. I just sat there. It was so much nicer than two cement blocks and a hole in the ground. Only upper-class families can afford toilets in Uganda.

We saw Pastor John Stocker from Resurrection Fellowship in Colorado preaching on Ugandan television. That was really cool. Of course, only upper-class Ugandans own televisions.

I'm glad I went to Africa, and I would go again. It was a sobering experience, but I made tons of friends. I loved the people and will remember them and what I learned from them the rest of my life.

Chapter 21

The Most Amazing Thing
Katherine, Ex-Inmate

The first time I tried to kill myself, I was eight-years old. I didn't know I was attempting suicide. All I knew was that aspirin took away pain. I didn't want my mom to beat me up again, and I didn't want more pain, so I ate an entire bottle of baby aspirin.

I survived the aspirin ordeal and managed to grow to adulthood in that abusive household. Despite my poor relationship with my mother, I was eventually married in the same New Jersey church where she married my father. My husband and I even lived in the same town.

It wasn't long before I was a mom as well as a wife. We had a son, Brian, and a daughter, Amanda. Our family was perfect, except for my husband's drug problem.

In 1989, we moved to Colorado to get away from the East Coast easy accessibility to drugs and alcohol. However, on New Year's Eve, my husband proudly showed me the score of cocaine he'd purchased and offered to share it with me while bringing in the New Year. That was the beginning of the end for us. We divorced in 1990.

I had a car accident in 1993 that resulted in a closed-head injury. I lost much of my memory as well as speech capabilities. I had to learn how to write again. Although I had taken college classes, after the accident I tested at a sixth-grade level, so I was forced to learn a lot of everyday functions over again. I still deal with some enduring effects of that accident.

Thirteen-year-old Amanda had to become a parent to her parent while I recovered. Brian, who was four years older than Amanda, couldn't help either of us, because I threw him out after we got into a vicious argument. That incident is just one of many bad moments I don't remember. I later learned that anger and erratic behavior are common to closed-head injuries.

Just prior to my accident, which happened the day before payday, I mailed several checks to pay bills. My plan was to deposit my paycheck the next day to cover the checks I'd written. But I never made it to the bank, so the checks started bouncing.

I couldn't comprehend what was happening, and I didn't have the stamina or the mental capacity to deal with my finances. Though it was not a deliberate action on my part, I ignored late notices and bank warnings. I just didn't know what to do. I had no clue. I was mentally younger than my daughter.

Even after I began to understand finances again, I wrote bad checks to feed us. I knew the money wasn't there. But each time, I thought, *I'll get a job soon, and I'll have the money to cover this check. We'll be okay.*

I would usually find a job; however, with my mental limitations, it would only last a month or so. Then I would be out of work for several months, and the depression I didn't realize I had would get worse.

Amanda and I started moving every couple of months. We'd rent a place until my bad checks caught up with us. Then we'd be evicted and find ourselves looking for somewhere else to live. I lied to landlord after landlord, and wrote bad check after bad check. I never meant to hurt anybody. I just did what I thought I had to do to get us by.

The depression got worse, and the aftereffects of the head injury also worsened. Sometimes, I'd stay in bed for days. It was just awful.

One day, I said to myself, *To heck with it,* and went shopping. I felt my daughter was being deprived of nice things, so I bought this, that and the other thing for the two of us. That's when the bad checks went beyond basic survival needs.

I wound up selling everything I bought. I don't know how many times I went through that routine. I had no support system, no guidance, no help. It was just me and Amanda and, eventually, Danny, my son's baby boy.

One morning when I was getting into my car to drive to yet another new job, police cars suddenly blocked my parking spot. The authorities arrested me, delivered Amanda to a friend's house, and took Danny to a foster home. I called relatives back East and pleaded until they scrounged up bail for me. That's when things began to seriously go downhill with my family, especially my mother.

I was devastated by my arrest. The depression went wild. I felt totally worthless. As soon as I was released, I started calling in prescriptions to different pharmacies. I knew the combination of medications required to overdose to the point there would be no waking me up, no pumping my stomach.

The last pharmacist I called recognized that I wasn't who I said I was and called the police. He saved my life, but the authorities didn't want to hear about my suicide plan. They didn't care about anything other than the fact that I had illegally obtained controlled substances, and that this was another felony to add to my growing list.

My aunt and my mother bailed me out again. Then my mother flew to Colorado, where she tricked Danny's biological mother into signing his guardianship over to her. Although Brian did not sign anything, we haven't seen Danny since.

Upon learning that I was looking at a 20-year sentence, I ran away to Wyoming. We went to Montana first, because there was a place there Amanda had always wanted to see. I let her do some barrel racing in Wyoming. And I found a good family to take care of her.

My plan was to return to LCDC and never come out. I wasn't going back to Colorado to clear things up, like I told Amanda and her new family. I was going to the place where I would die.

When I turned myself in, I told LCDC officials, "I don't want to go to court for bond. I'm not bailing myself out."

I told them I was staying put until things were cleared up. If it meant I had to sit in jail for months, that was what I was going to do. It didn't really matter to me, because I knew I would never leave the county jail.

They put me on suicide watch and had me talk with counselors. I was aloof. One of the counselors finally said, "I think you need to talk with Chaplain Donna Roth."

I said, "Fine." Whatever they asked me to do, I did. But my mind was busy working on the perfect suicide plan.

So they sent Donna up. She talked to me in a nice, calm voice for about 45 minutes. Then I said, "Who are you, and what church are you from?" She explained a little more about who she was, but nothing registered.

Donna asked me if I believed in God. I said, "Yeah, I grew up Lutheran. What difference does it make?"

I was curt, yet Donna kept coming back. She brought me Scriptures when she visited. She didn't just hand me the list and tell me to read the verses in my cell. Instead, she had me read them right then and there with her, or she read them aloud to me.

What she said started to sink in. I thought, *Well, maybe there is something more to life.* For the first time, I began to think that maybe things could be different in my life. Maybe I wasn't a complete failure.

One day, she asked me if I wanted to accept God into my heart. I said I did, and we prayed together. I felt a little bit better about myself. Donna kept coming to visit me. It was a process.

I was in LCDC for four months. Then I went to the Work Release program for four months. After that, I was transferred to the Halfway House, where I tried again to kill myself. That experience was the most amazing thing that ever happened to me.

I hadn't been at the Halfway House 30 days, when I broke one of the rules by being late to work. I was given the maximum punishment. That meant I couldn't do anything but go to work and to certain Community Corrections programs for the next 21 days.

For me, that was the end of it. If I couldn't handle a simple rule like getting to work on time, I would never get out of the Halfway House. I thought, *I'm just a total screw-up. I'll never make it through here. There's nothing on the outside for me. Even my daughter no longer needs me.*

I packed up my things, put all of my business in order, and returned my tickets for Timberline Church's Passion Play. I had everything all planned and ready to go, but I never told a soul I was going to kill myself.

One evening, after all three of my roommates were in bed, I went into the bathroom and took a hot shower. Then I picked up the plastic wastebasket liner I'd swiped, looked at myself in the mirror, and said, "Katherine, for once in your life, you're going to do something right."

I put the bag over my head, twisted it around my neck, and knotted it up tight. Knowing the warm shower would relax me enough to put me to sleep, I curled up on a towel on the bathroom floor and began to feel myself go out. There was no lock on the bathroom door, but my roommates were all sleeping, so I wasn't worried about anybody coming in.

Suddenly, there was a loud pounding on the door, an awful noise. The sound literally jumped me to my feet. I ripped the plastic bag off my head, thinking, *Oh, no, staff!* But no one walked in, despite the fact that I'd heard a booming bang that took me directly from unconsciousness to my feet. I know I was out for at least a couple seconds, because there is a space of time I don't remember.

After a minute or so, I poked my head out the bathroom door and peeked into the bedroom. The room was pitch-black dark. Not one roommate was awake. I stood there thinking, *What just happened?*

Finally, I dried myself, put on my pajamas, and lay down on my bed. As I lay there trying to figure out what was going on, I prayed, *OK, Lord, if you see me through the night, and I wake up in the morning, I'll rethink all this.*

I learned later that a group of Freedom Fellowship volunteers had been praying for me at the very time I heard the bang. They had sensed I might be planning to kill myself that night.

After that, things got really good for me at the Halfway House. And I started going to the Road to Freedom mental health class, which is a self-help group. I was also given a psychological test that indicated I was still dealing with the head injury. In addition, the test showed borderline personality disorder and major depression.

God has put a very good counselor in my life. She's a Christian who's worked with me free of charge since my insurance ran out. She's seen me come from a black hole, where there was no light at all, to where I am now.

I have flashbacks, but I believe God is using them to heal me. I don't stay in the downslides as long as I used to. Although a downslide can happen quickly, I'm able to reverse it almost as quickly, much faster than I used to.

I still struggle with the fact that I don't deserve God's grace and mercy. People tell me no one deserves God's love; that's why Christ died on the cross. I'm up to 90 percent of the time believing that as a fact, but there's still 10 percent of me that battles with accepting God's love, grace and mercy.

My son and my daughter and I are working through family issues from the accident—the changes in me, the changes in them. God is restoring our relationships. It's slow. Sometimes I get frustrated and upset, but it's coming around.

I'm learning to trust people. Trust has been a hard issue for me. If someone else has a problem, there's nothing they can tell me that will shock or hurt me. Yet, when it comes to me confiding in others, I struggle. I'm afraid of losing the friendship we have. I might tell them the one thing that would push them away from me. I'm too afraid to take that chance.

Shirley taught me that it's okay and safe to have a female as a friend. I never had female friends before because of my unhealthy relationship with my mother. I guess that's part of what I've spent my life searching for—a real relationship with my mom.

There have been many times when I pictured myself hanging off a cliff with either Shirley or Edith from Freedom Fellowship holding onto me, because I couldn't reach my hand to Christ. They hold on until I can make the connection for myself.

Needless to say, I feel a dedication toward Freedom Fellowship and Donna and all the volunteers. I've been trying to give back what they gave me. They've been a great support system. When I'm with the volunteers or in the support group with others who have been incarcerated, I don't ever feel like a criminal. Freedom Fellowship always makes me feel like a first-class citizen.

Chapter 22

It Doesn't Get Any Better than This
Shawn, Ex-Inmate

My mom began taking me and my brother to church in Loveland when I was in the 5th grade. That's when I accepted Christ into my life. As a teenager, I was involved with my youth group and in plays at church. Then I stopped going to church and started smoking pot and hanging out with a different crowd.

I was a very business-minded individual, even in high school, so it didn't take me long to see the advantage of selling marijuana. There was a big ring of us, nine guys altogether, who got busted for selling dope on campus when I was a junior.

Because I was a juvenile, all they could do was give me probation and make me read books and give book reports. That punishment didn't faze me. I continued to smoke and sell pot and party. I had plenty of money and a nice car.

Despite all the trouble I got into, my parents stuck with me through thick and thin. I thank God my mom is a prayer warrior. I really put her and Dad through the wringer.

Just one example: After high school, they took me on a trip to New Orleans, which is called the "Big Easy" on the streets. Whoever named it that wasn't kidding. The first night there, I dealt dope in a neighborhood that looked like something out of a movie. It was a total "projects" area—even had cars up on blocks. I was the only white guy, but I sold some crack and some dope, and I bought some dope.

The next day, I went back to the same spot and was doing a deal in a back alley, when a black Ford Taurus came roaring up beside us. The Taurus jerked to a halt as two big black guys with medallions bouncing on their chests jumped out. I took off bookin' across a four-lane highway and ran right in front of a car, which barely missed me.

It wasn't long before I began to tire and slow down. The men were catching up to me, so I stopped and ducked, expecting them to fly past me. Then I planned to double back and escape. Instead, 300 pounds of muscle ground me into the dirt. The guy grabbed my neck, jerked me up, and slammed me against a wall with one hand. With the other, he shoved a Mac 10 against my head.

Thinking I had swallowed some crack, he kept screaming in my face, "Spit it out! Spit it out!"

There was a guy across the street painting a church. I can remember him yelling, "Someone call the cops! They're robbing him!"

Just then, the Taurus screeched to a stop beside us, and the other cop hurtled out, hollering, "We *are* cops!"

Within moments, I was on my way to jail. All the way there, I kept thinking, *Ha-ha, I'm only 17. They can't touch me. I'm a minor.* I was soon to learn, however, that a 17-year-old is considered an adult in New Orleans.

It was probably 110 degrees in that jail, and it smelled really bad. The only item on the menu was grits. I had to talk a trusty into bringing me some canned peaches just to have something familiar to eat. Although I was incarcerated in New

Orleans for only 24 hours, I remember every single moment with clarity.

I was the only white guy in the entire jail, but the other inmates liked me because I could tell stories. One guy, who looked like Mike Tyson—even the tooth, wanted to be my friend and give me pointers. "Man," he said, "you went over to those Fifth Ward projects? I don't even go there."

I called the hotel and asked the desk clerk to tell my parents I was in jail. I remember how bad I felt when I walked into the courtroom and saw my mom and dad sitting there looking so distraught. Since my bond was set at $300,000, they had to hire a lawyer, who got me out on a $13,000 bond.

After high school, I started a landscaping business, which I operated for a year. I also began using and selling cocaine. When my girlfriend decided to go to college in Phoenix, I sold the business and went with her to school. I thought it would be a good place for me to start over, to regroup.

Phoenix is a border town. A lot of drugs go through there. Within a week, I discovered that my next door neighbor was a big dope dealer. I partnered with another guy and together we sold massive amounts of marijuana, plus we used and sold methamphetamine.

I quit going to school. The only real job I ever worked in Phoenix lasted two weeks. My relationship with my girlfriend, whom I had dated all through high school, turned sour.

I found myself in some pretty scary scenarios in Phoenix. I had guns pointed at my head more than once. I have a dual scar on my chin from the time I was jumped by nine guys and kicked in the chin. They took my dope, but I managed to hang onto the $3000 I had in my hand. About a month later, my chin was split again when I got into another fight.

One morning around 3:00 a.m., I heard a knock on the door. When I went to answer it, I thought, *Oh, I forgot my gun.* So I walked over to the coffee table, picked up the gun and opened the door. All the while, I was thinking, *What am I doing? This is crazy. I would never need a gun in Loveland.*

Shortly after that incident, due to a deal that went bad with some White Nation bikers, I moved to San Diego. Within a couple days, I was hustling dope in that city. Then I went to live with a buddy in Sacramento. I tried to get a job there, and I tried to be straight, but I didn't like Sacramento.

So I moved back to Loveland, where one of my old buddies was dealing drugs on a very large scale with a guy who was importing dope from Mexico. It didn't take long for the cops to figure out what I was up to. By then I was more into partying and using dope than selling it, but I still sold some.

I lived in motel rooms, a different motel room every night to avoid the cops. Almost every night, I had people in my room partying all night long. At one motel, I got into a fight with someone who owed me for a cocaine deal. I wasn't a big drinker, but I happened to be pretty drunk that night and caused enough of a ruckus that the cops were called.

I ended up in Larimer County Detention Center for two weeks for possession of cocaine. While I was in jail, God used Donna to remind me of my relationship with him. I started praying again. "Lord," I said, "get me out of this mess, and I won't do drugs again." I was able to pay my bail and bond out of jail within two weeks. God kept his end of the deal, but I figured I deserved to celebrate, so that's what I did.

Three months later, I sold a friend a large amount of marijuana. When I thought he would be ready for more, I called him. "Hey, are you ready for another supply?"

"I don't have enough money."

"So, what did you do with all your marijuana?"

"I smoked some and gave some away."

That's strange, I thought. *I sold you a lot of marijuana. You should have had plenty to smoke and to sell.*

From then on, he kept trying to introduce me to his "friend." But I kept saying, "I don't want to know your friend. I know enough people as it is. If your friend wants dope, he can go to you, and you can come to me." I didn't realize it, but the "friend" was an undercover cop.

Three months later, he called again. "Hey, our friend is out of town. Can you set me up with some meth?"

I said, "Okay," and we arranged a meeting place. The cops were with him, but they didn't detain me. They just put out a warrant for my arrest. It wasn't long before I was picked up.

When my bondsman called me in jail, he said, "What did you do? You have nine felony charges. They're not even issuing a bond. No amount of money will get you out right now."

Finally, a bond was set, but it was huge. I slowly accepted the fact that jail was to be my residence for a while.

Because I was a smart-mouthed punk, I was locked down often, spending 23 hours a day in my cell. My cellmate's pastor visited him and gave him a New Testament. I started reading it. I remember reading the parables and reading about Jesus. When I was no longer locked down, I joined a group of guys who had a daily Bible study within our pod.

I happened to know what they were talking about, because I had just read it in my cellmate's Bible. So I shared insights and questions I had about the passage. They were shocked. I was the last person they thought would know anything about the Bible.

I went to every church service offered in the jail. That's how I got to know Pastor Dave. Something in him struck a tone within me and vice versa. He used to come in on his own time just to get to know me better. I rededicated my life to Christ, asking him to transform me and renew me, to make me like him.

After LCDC, I was sent to the Halfway House for six months and started going to Northgate Church on the Rock because I knew Pastor Dave. I was even asked to be an usher. But six months in the Halfway House weighs on a person when there are 65 other residents who aren't interested in godly things.

I started pushing the limits again, going out on Friday nights with old friends and drinking—just being an idiot. It wasn't long before I ran into a friend from jail who sold me a whole bunch of coke. To make a long story short, I regressed, which was devastating to me. I knew the truth. I had experienced the glory of God.

I ended up back in jail. That was hard. I'm not normally an emotional person, but I was that week. I remember being on my knees, praying and crying, "Lord, I know I screwed up. I don't know what you're going to do with me here, but I do know your Word says you work all things for your good."

I spent most of my time reading the Bible and praying. I miss that time now. I was able to pray three hours a day and spend the rest of the day reading the Bible and getting filled up with God's Word.

This time I wasn't a smart-mouthed punk. I was made a trusty due to good behavior and moved over to the minimum security unit. That was nice. I got involved with Freedom Fellowship and the other church services and just kept growing spiritually. God began to reveal to me my gift of teaching the Word. I started leading some of the Bible studies within the pods.

One night, God gave me a message for the Bible study with an awesome theme associated with the beer commercial that says "It doesn't get any better than this." Normally, five or six guys attended the group. But by the end of the message, there must have been 30 guys standing around listening. I just praised God.

Then I was sent to the Colorado Department of Corrections, where I was in a cell with a CRIP, a gang banger from Denver. Each night, the guards would throw plastic bags under the doors of those people who were getting shipped out the next day. That meant, *you're moving on*, so *pack your bags*.

Neither of us were getting bags. I prayed about it and felt the Lord telling me, "You guys aren't getting bags until one of you gets saved." I knew I was already saved, so I led this CRIP, this guy who'd been involved in drive-by shootings, to the Lord.

Soon, I was moved to the Territorial Prison, a very old prison that must have been built in the late 1800s. I was there for a couple of months waiting to go into the boot camp program. Under God's leading, I organized a small Bible study at that prison and did a lot of witnessing.

Boot camp turned out to be the hardest thing I ever had to do, physically and emotionally. They are not joking at boot camp. The program is so intense judges reconsider the sentences of those who graduate.

The first week is called "hell week," and it's pretty darn close to that. There was some "weeping and gnashing of teeth" going on, for sure. The leaders lighten up later, but the plan the first month is to break people down. The plan the first week is to break them down *fast*.

It's intentionally strenuous and emotionally difficult. I couldn't sleep the first night. Over and over, I asked myself the same questions: *What did I do? Why did I choose boot camp? Why am I here? How can I do this?*

The next night, I was fast asleep as soon as I hit the bunk. But I was awakened all too soon by revelry, along with sound of trash can lids banging near my ears. Despite the trauma, boot camp was an awesome time in my life. It taught me discipline; it taught me team work.

I had opportunities to witness to so many guys there. They got to see Christ in me. Boot camp brings a whole bunch of different people together—gang bangers, thieves, alcoholics, druggies, you name it—and forces them to work as a team.

You can imagine the conflicts that arose. I thank God I was able to set a godly example in the midst of the bickering and fighting. One gang banger even noticed I was never involved in the quarrels within the platoon.

Graduation was great, the first time in my life I'd ever accomplished anything positive. I'd been kicked out of high school the last day of my senior year for being stoned, so I didn't graduate with my class, although I got a diploma. It felt good to graduate from boot camp.

The whole time I was at the camp, I prayed I would get intensive supervised probation with an ankle monitor. When I told people what I was praying for, they said, "Shawn, you're crazy if you think you're not going to get sent back to the Halfway House." But two months after graduation, I was put on ISP.

The judge said I needed to be on ISP for a year. In three months, however, I was off ISP and on regular probation. My re-sentencing was for five years adult probation. Praise God, it's been three years now, and I'm on the most minimal probation.

After I was released, I attended Front Range Community College for two years. The turnaround in my life was amazing. I received the Dean's Scholarship for maintaining a 3.8 grade point average the first year. The second year, I had a 3.4 GPA and received the Colorado Scholars Scholarship.

I also started helping with the college ministry at church. After a while, the Lord told me, "Someday you will lead this ministry."

I said, "Wow, Lord. That's awesome."

About three months passed. One night before I went to bed, I prayed, "Lord, I know you told me it's going to be my ministry. Give me the patience to wait, or if someone needs to make a move, so be it." Within a week, the leader told me he was ready to step down, and I was given the college director position.

The college ministry is a blessing to me. I enjoy spending time with people. I've learned to love individuals and understand where they've been. Lately, I've been hanging out with a guy who lives at the Halfway House. I know where he's at in life. I can relate to his circumstances and encourage him.

My life is the exact opposite of what it used to be. I didn't work when I was a dealer. Now I work a full-time job. I used to carry guns and sell dope. Now I lead the college ministry at church. I used to live for myself and party all the time. Now I'm married and share life with my beautiful wife, Sarah.

You couldn't pay me all the money in the world to go back to the lifestyle I lived in my past. My life was empty. I was always searching for something, but I didn't know what it was. I was never satisfied.

When I began to develop my relationship with God, I experienced a peace I'd never had before. There was a new level of truth and completeness in my life. In my drug days, even if I smoked the best marijuana in the world, I didn't attain peace.

Peace is a huge thing for me, because there is no peace for a hustler. Life passed me by. I was always in a hurry, always late, always worried, always watching my back. Now I enjoy life and make the most of each day.

I enjoy the miracle of my own life. I enjoy the life I see in other people. I enjoy knowing every individual is a creation of God, and I enjoy being able to love others because of that knowledge. I once lived in bondage and deception, but now I live in truth and love.

Chapter 23

Adult Church
Chaplain Donna Roth, Founder and Director

One summer evening, Edith and I set up a Freedom Fellowship information display at a "Praise in the Park" concert. When we finished, we asked God to send someone special to our table. It wasn't long before a nice lady came up and began to look at our brochures and newsletters.

"Are you interested in volunteering in the jails and prisons?" I asked her.

"Yes, I am," she said. "But I have to wait until I retire, because I'm a sex offender probation officer."

I said, "I want to talk with you!"

I've grieved for years because ex-inmates with sex offense charges cannot attend church services due to the presence of children. I shared with her how my heart ached for those who became Christians in prison or jail, but who were not allowed to attend church after they were released.

The woman said she agreed with me and that she would talk to the other probation officers about the situation. The very next day, she left a phone message saying if we wanted to start an adults-only church, the sex offender system would sanction it, because they trust Freedom Fellowship.

I said, "Praise God!" and immediately began making arrangements for an adult church. Within a few short weeks, our unique church had its first service on a Sunday afternoon.

One ex-offender and several volunteers attended, with much rejoicing.

After three months of weekly services, we now have five to seven ex-inmates who participate regularly, plus several other adults and some Freedom Fellowship volunteers. Our average attendance is 15. The church is growing slowly, but surely. God is blessing us.

Pastor Mike from Father's House Ministries speaks three out of four services each month. On the fourth Sunday, we have a guest speaker. Different music teams join us each week to lead worship. We also pray together as a group.

God has already answered prayers for members of our little church. Some have found jobs. Others have been healed of sickness. We've all been encouraged. We also pray for the justice system as it relates to sex offenders.

Mike and the other teachers provide wonderful, positive teaching. I've watched the men change. When they first come, they walk in with their heads down, because they are so ashamed. They start out sad, shy and quiet and then become outgoing and happy when they're offered faith and hope and realize they have a great future in Christ.

Father's House Ministries is letting us use their facilities. We don't advertise the Freedom Fellowship Adult Church. We just trust God to bring in the people he wants to join us. We don't focus on the past or on ex-inmate offenses. Instead, we have normal church services, so they can experience what they'd experience if they were allowed to go to any other church.

The Lord says sin is sin and that we are not to judge one sin over the other. However, our sex offenders are constantly judged, worse than murderers are judged. I feel the

Lord is telling us that if we will come together in our little church and pray, things are going to change for that particular group of people. God loves them, and so do the Freedom Fellowship volunteers.

The adult church concept may be a new frontier in America. I pray other cities and states will follow suit. This type of ministry could become very big in our country.

I am so privileged to watch people who feel like the lowest of the low be filled with God's power and joy and become what the Lord has created them to be—vessels for his glory. We serve an awesome and amazing God who sets the captives free!

For information about adult church services, please see our website: http://www.freedom-fellowship.org; or contact us at:

970-310-5711

info@freedom-fellowship.org

Freedom Fellowship
PO Box 726
Fort Collins, CO 80522

Chapter 24

There Is No Tomorrow
Steve, Ex-Inmate

My grandma and grandpa both died when I was in the third grade. I loved them very much, and I loved to go to their farm. I liked to climb on the hay and play with the chickens and the bulls. After they died, I noticed there was something different about my family. Something had changed. That's when my dad and mom filed for their first divorce. My parents were alcoholics, which caused a lot of trauma in my family. They eventually got back together and tried to work things out but ended up getting another divorce.

My brother, Don, was married by then. My sister, Leanne, and I went to live with my mom. We lived in some bad places. Sometimes we had to live with aunts and uncles. We were so poor we stopped celebrating Christmas.

My mom eventually met a guy in a bar who became my stepfather. He was also an alcoholic. I saw him beat my mom several times. When I stood up to him, I got my butt kicked, which was nothing new to me. More than once my Dad had beat me from one end of the house to the other with his fists.

About a year after I graduated from high school, I moved to California, because my brother and his wife lived there. I got a good job, but there was still something missing in my life. One night, when I was sitting by the apartment pool, this woman from the complex came over to me and said, "I've been watching you."

I said, "Oh, have you?"

"Yeah, you've slimmed down. You've lost some weight. I'd kinda like to get to know you."

"That's awful nice of you," I said," but you didn't want anything to do with me before. Why do you want anything to do with me now?"

Despite that comment, she stayed, and we talked a bit. Then she said, "Why don't you come upstairs with me?"

We went to her apartment, where she offered me cocaine—first time I ever did drugs in my life. I was 21-years old. I thought, *I could really like this.*

Later, after a year of using cocaine, I looked in the mirror and was frightened by what I saw. "You've got to do something about this," I told myself.

I called my sister, who was living in Wichita with her husband, Leroy. I was crying, hard. "I need to get away from here," I told her. "It's killing me."

She knew what I was talking about. My brother had noticed the changes in me and told her what he suspected. She said, "If you can find a way to get here, you're welcome to stay with us until you get on your feet again."

Shortly after that, I ran into one of my friends from Iowa. He said he was about to head back home. I asked, "Are you going through Kansas?"

"Yeah," he said, "I go right through Wichita."

I did better in Kansas. I found a job and tried to be responsible. One morning, my brother-in-law took me to a car lot and told me to choose the car I wanted.

I said, "What?"

"You find the car you want, and I'll pay for it. You've been doing good. I don't mind helping somebody who's trying."

So I picked out a car, and he wrote a check for it. When I got home, I told my sister what Leroy had done for me. "That's the way he is," she said. "He's proud of you for trying."

Not long after that, my stepsister, Kathy, took me to a place called Porky's. It was a unique bar, because they had telephones in the booths, so you could call other tables and talk. We were sitting there visiting with each other, when the phone rang. I said, "Are you going to get that?"

Kathy said, "Why don't you get it?"

"No, you get it."

She picked it up, listened and said, "It's for you."

"What?"

I talked a little bit, and then this girl stood up at another table. "We're over here," she called. "We'd like you and your girlfriend to come over and join us."

I laughed, knowing Kathy was my stepsister, not my girlfriend. "Okay, I guess we can."

We walked over and introduced ourselves. The girl's name was Trina. She said, "Why don't you and your girlfriend sit down."

I laughed again, but we sat down.

Then music started. Trina wanted to dance. "Do you think your girlfriend would mind if we danced?" she asked.

I laughed.

She said, "What's so funny?"

"Kathy is my stepsister, not my girlfriend."

Trina and I had a good time dancing together. When I looked into her eyes, I felt something different, something I'd never felt before in my life—something very good. We were married within six months. My mom adored Trina. Everybody adored her. She was just that type. Soon we had a baby boy we named Jeremy. Trina already had a son from a previous marriage. I was content and happy with our little family.

Then Trina's grandmother died. She lived next door to us, and her death was very upsetting to my wife and her parents. Trina's mom and dad decided there was nothing left in Wichita to keep them from moving to Arkansas, where they owned property. They wanted us to go with them, so we did.

About a year later, Trina began to have really bad headaches. When she put her glasses on, however, the headaches eased up. I told her, "You probably need to have your prescription changed," and picked up the phone book to find an optometrist.

The day of her appointment, I received a call at work: "This is the eye clinic. We've just admitted your wife to the hospital."

"What's going on?" I asked.

The doctor said, "I'm concerned because there seems to be some kind of blockage."

At the hospital, they found a brain tumor the size of a grapefruit. I called the one person who was always there for me, my sister. But after I said hello, I was too upset to talk.

Leanne said, "Steve, what's wrong? It's Trina, isn't it?"

"How did you know?"

"I felt it."

"Trina has a brain tumor," I told Leanne. "They're going to operate on Thursday." Leanne came immediately.

Trina was in surgery for 18 hours. They were able to get most of the tumor, but there were areas they couldn't get to. I was the first to see her after the surgery. She looked like she'd gone too many rounds with Mohammed Ali. Her eyes were bruised, and her face was swollen. Her beautiful, long brown hair had been shaved off.

It was hard for me to look at her, but I had to be strong. Waiting by her bedside was the most difficult thing I've ever done. Somehow, I made it through. Within a couple of days, Trina was sitting up in bed. She was a strong woman.

One day, we were sitting together in her hospital room, just the two of us, and she asked me, "How long do I have to live?"

Her doctor had given me an estimate of the time she had left. "But," he said, "one thing I never do is tell my patients how long they have to live. If I do, they might give up and die."

I told Trina, "I need to go smoke a cigarette," and went outside.

Her family and my sister came to talk with me. "Trina asked me how long she has to live," I told them. "What do I tell her?"

I looked at Trina's mom, who was so close to her daughter. She said, "I don't know what to tell you, Steve."

I looked at Leanne. For the first time in her life, my sister didn't have an answer for me. "I can't tell you. That's something you're going to have to do yourself."

So I smoked my cigarette and thought. Finally, I went back upstairs. When I walked in, Trina said, "Are you going to answer my question?"

"Yeah." I sat down beside her, took her hand, and looked her in the eyes. "We're just going to take this day by day," I said. "What becomes of it, becomes of it." That was the best answer I could give her. Trina seemed satisfied with my response.

She was released the following Tuesday. We were new to that small Arkansas town and hardly knew a soul. Even so, people from different churches started coming over with food and money. They just kept coming. They paid our rent and our utility bills and other bills. I couldn't believe it.

Trina soon began chemotherapy and radiation. It took a toll on her, but she was a fighter, who was still there to be my wife and to mother our boys. I told her, "We've been through the worst it could ever get, and we made it. What does that tell you, Trina? It tells me our love for each other is really strong."

Then Trina started losing her hair again. Her speech became slurred, and I saw other signs the doctor had warned me about. I thought, *I can't do this.*

At night, when I lay in bed holding Trina close, I could hear the doctor saying, "When it happens, she'll go to sleep and not wake up." I couldn't live with that knowledge, so I started doing drugs again, my way of running from my problems.

I told Trina, "I can't watch somebody I really care about die and not be able to do a damn thing about it. I know I'm being selfish, but that's the way it is."

Trina finally had to make a choice. Fighting for her own life while I was throwing mine away was more than she could handle. We divorced about nine months after the tumor was discovered.

When I signed the divorce papers, I also signed away my rights to my son. Trina didn't want the boys separated. I signed away everything. I have no visitation rights and haven't seen Jeremy in almost 10 years. I don't know whether Trina is alive or not. I regret a lot of things I've done in my life, but leaving Trina and Jeremy is the thing I regret the most.

I moved to Fort Collins to be near my sister and started in on the drugs again. They kept me from facing reality. I didn't want to deal with the loneliness. As long as I had dope, I had women and I had power. People were paying attention to me, but they were around me for all the wrong reasons. I knew that, but I didn't care.

Then I started doing methamphetamine. Eventually, I manufactured the drug. When you make meth, you have to snort it, smoke it, and slam it to test it, because if you put a bad batch out on the streets, it could kill somebody. I would rather kill myself.

Sometimes I was high for more than a month at a time. I didn't eat or sleep—just drank Gatorade. I weighed around 110 pounds. I was way out of control, slamming anywhere from 30 to 70 cc's every two-to-three hours.

One night, I had a "cook" heating on the stove while I showered. When I got out, the phone rang. It was Patty, the person I was staying with at the time. "The cops are here looking for you, Steve," she said. "They're right outside."

DEA agents, a SWAT team, and several members of the sheriff's department—probably about a dozen officers altogether—had surrounded the place. Their high-powered rifles were aimed at every possible exit. They wanted me, but they were also planning to bust Patty for being an accessory to a meth lab. I couldn't let that happen, so I tore the whole thing down and stashed it in a well under the floor of the house.

I filled up some syringes with the remaining couple of grams of meth and stuck them all in my arms. Then I just sat there, holding a knife in front of me, trying to decide what to do. The cops kept calling and bothering me, which irritated me.

But then, something clicked in my head. I thought, *You put out your cry for help. The help is here.* So I told the officer on the phone, "Give me an hour, and I'll be out."

"No, you need to come out now."

"Don't push me. You give me an hour, and I'll come out."

"Okay, you've got an hour."

During that 60 minutes, I did some serious soul searching. I told myself, *If I go out there, I'll end up in prison. On the other hand ...* I stared at the knife. *I have an easy way out. Which one do I do?*

Actually, the knife looked like the best alternative at that moment. But I got to thinking, *It's not really the easy way out, because I'll have to answer for what I've done.* Deep down inside, I knew I would have to answer to God, and that knowledge scared me.

After an hour of debate, I stood up and walked out the front door, blood trickling down my emaciated arms. I felt the tension in the air, and I also sensed the gun barrels tracking my every step.

One officer walked up to me. "You got a meth lab in there?" he asked.

"I don't know what you're talking about."

"By the looks of your arms," he said, "you don't have any dope left. Get in the car."

Before I went to prison, I told the judge, "I'm a drug addict, a heavy user. I started doing needles, and I really like it. I know I'm going to go to prison, which is fine. I probably need that. I need something hard. But when I get out of prison, I don't have any place to go."

The judge sat back in his chair. "What do you have in mind?"

"I would like to go to Larimer County Day Care, as I call it, until there is an opening in the Halfway House." He agreed to that. He knew I needed help, that I couldn't handle a return to the streets as soon I was released.

After a year in prison, I was transferred to LCDC. While I was there, I got into some trouble and was put into the "hole," which is a 23-hour a day lock down for three months.

Donna Roth checked in on me now and then to see how I was doing. I was really gruff with her. "I know what you're doing. I'm fine. I don't need you."

I kicked her to the curb, but Donna is an amazing person. She doesn't give up, because she knows what's happening inside a person's heart. She kept bugging me to do some reading. Finally, I read a book she brought me called "Free on the Inside." It was like déjà vu, because much of what happened in that book had transpired in my life.

As I finished reading "Free on the Inside," I broke down and fell to my knees. "I've always chosen the wrong road, God," I sobbed. "Yet, for some reason, I'm still alive. This is me. You know me. Let's see what you've got. Let's try it and see. I can't guarantee I'm going to be the ultimate Christian, because that's not me, but I'll give it a shot."

I bawled for days. I needed that time, and I began to feel something different inside me. It was like a new spark, like something was happening. I started talking with Donna.

When I got out of solitary, Donna still came to see me. I went to some of the religious services, but nothing clicked, so I asked Donna for a Bible. She brought me one in modern English I could understand. I read a lot in my new Bible and highlighted a bunch of stuff in it. I read all the passages about angels. I like angels. They are so cool.

I also read other passages, like the one about the prodigal son. That story is the story of my relationship with my sister. Every time I came back, Leanne welcomed me with open arms. It gave me a really eerie feeling to read that story.

One Friday night, I heard there was a religious service at the jail. I said, "I ain't goin' to another one of those. I won't get nothin' out of it."

But something told me, *You'd better go to this one.*

The service was supposed to be for the women. However, there weren't very many women there, so they let the guys join in. The speaker's sermon was about the woman at the well.

Just as the man started to preach, he turned toward me. There must have been an arrow over my head, because he looked at me and instantly changed his sermon text. I think it was from the book of Jeremiah, something like, "If you don't wash your hands of this and this and this, you'll die." I felt like it was directed straight at me.

I couldn't turn away. Afterward, I got up and started to walk toward the speaker. After only a couple steps, I collapsed. He asked, "Are you alright?" as he helped me up.

I said, "I don't know. I can barely breathe. There's something going on in me."

The guy looked into my eyes. "You're experiencing what I've been hoping and praying for."

"What is it?"

"The Holy Spirit. Just let go. Let him fill you."

I headed back to my cell but collapsed at the bottom of the stairs. My good friend Wally helped me up to my cell and onto my bunk.

"Are you okay?" he asked.

"No, I'm not. There's something going on, Wally, and I don't understand it."

"Just relax for a while."

I couldn't relax. I felt goose bumps all over me, and I was so excited, I couldn't sit still. It felt like fireworks were going off inside me. I got up and started walking laps, around and around the walkway.

Finally, I stopped by a window, looked up at the full moon high in the night sky and said, "God, if this is what I think it is, I want it all. Don't just tease me. I want it all."

Suddenly, I felt like I was being flushed with pure water, like I was getting cleansed and filtered. I said, "God, I want more of it."

That was the best high I ever experienced, and I wasn't doped up. It took me three days to recover. My body felt like I'd been run over by a truck. When I saw Donna a few days later, she knew immediately what had happened to me.

After seven or eight months at LCDC, I was sent to the Halfway House for eight months. I've been living in my own place for a couple years, but I'm still vulnerable. I'm still fresh. I'm not used to this world.

Put me in the world behind bars, and I can handle that. I can adapt to that society, a world populated with people similar to me, people who live on the edge. I feel more accepted there than on the outside.

My drug issue is a daily battle. There is no tomorrow. I only know that *today* I choose not to use drugs. I have to live one day at a time. Tomorrow may never come.

I make the choice not to use drugs *today* because of God's love for me and my love for him. I also make that choice because I'm learning to love myself and learning to appreciate the freedom I have on the outside to enjoy the world God created.

Chapter 25

I Could Have Danced All Night
Edith, Former Board Member

My father abandoned our family when I was a young child. Years later, at his funeral, I learned he'd lived on Larimer Street, Denver's downtown skid row, for some time. I was 35 years old when he died.

Not long after his funeral, I joined a group that ministered to street people in downtown Denver. The organization folded within a few months, so I started praying for something similar to do because I enjoyed street ministry.

One evening, I visited a church that featured the Freedom Fellowship prison ministry during the service. The more I listened to the music and testimonies of ex-inmates, chaplains and volunteers, the more God tugged at my heart. I'd never before thought of going into jails or prisons to minister.

It took only one visit to the Larimer County Detention Center to hook me. I became a regular volunteer at the jail. Then I started going to prisons with Freedom Fellowship. Volunteering filled the big hole left in my heart after my marriage ended in divorce. As I focused outside of myself and started helping others, I began to heal. I also made lots of new friends.

My main function at LCDC is to be an encourager through visiting and interacting with inmates. I enjoy playing volleyball with the women and talking and praying with both the women and the men. I've also gotten to know ex-inmates through the support group.

I help Freedom Fellowship in various ways, including calling local pastors to ask if we can do presentations at their churches. When we go before a congregation, we show a video or have ex-inmates tell how Freedom Fellowship was an important part of their re-entry into society. Volunteers tell about their involvement with the ministry.

We let the church groups know we need prayer warriors and volunteers. We also ask for cookies and books for the prison weekends. Besides support people for the seminars, we're always looking for individuals who can speak and/or lead worship.

Later, I call those who indicate an interest in volunteering to find out more about them. I pass that information on to Ginny, who matches those people with the current needs of the ministry. It's quite a coordination effort.

We have prayer meetings for the ministry every Monday evening. Anyone can come—volunteers, ex-inmates, pastors, people wanting to learn more about Freedom Fellowship. We also have get-togethers throughout the year for ex-inmates and their families, and volunteers and their families, including picnics and a Christmas party.

Twelve of us went to Uganda last summer to hold services at several prisons. When Ugandan men are imprisoned, the only clothes they have are the ones they were wearing when arrested. They're never given more clothing. We saw men with just blankets wrapped around their bodies. We saw many who wore only threadbare remnants of shirts, a few strings stretched across their thin chests. The men do not receive hygiene supplies or medicine, and their diet consists of a bowl of beans twice a day.

We were only allowed into the courtyards of the prisons. We did not go inside the facilities, but we knew they were large, with many inmates. We were told that prisoners who have sentences longer than a year usually don't make it out of the prison because they die of AIDS, malaria, tuberculosis, typhoid, or some other terrible disease.

The inmates were happy to see outsiders. Some of them had never seen white people before. If they knew the songs our African and American musicians played, they sang along with us. Most Africans know English, but we provided an interpreter for those who didn't.

We also visited a women's facility located on the shore of beautiful Lake Victoria, the second largest lake in the world. No fence or wall blocks the shoreline, because the lake is infested with man-eating creatures. No one ever tries to escape.

The facility has a farm, where the women produce vegetables to eat. They also raise cattle for meat, and they grow flowers. Some of the women even have nursing babies with them in prison.

We noticed the morale was higher in the women's prisons than in the men's. Someone told Donna the women's crimes are usually less detestable. As a result, they're treated better. Female inmates are given uniforms, so adequate clothing is not an issue for them.

We provided music, teaching and testimonies at the Ugandan prisons and at the crusades. When we asked if anyone wanted to be born again, many came forward. When we asked if anyone wanted prayer for healing or hurts in their lives, crowds would come.

Through an interpreter, we asked, "Where do you hurt?" Most people had congestion in their lungs. So many came for prayer we couldn't talk with them one-on-one. We just touched them and prayed for each person.

The first week we were there, we led a crusade in Impala from 5:00 until 9:00 each evening. People rode bicycles or walked to the crusade. Our group was given chairs to sit on, but the locals stood for three hours, which was very humbling to us.

The meetings started out with the American and the African music teams playing together. The praise and worship was awesome. I had fun dancing with the African people and could have danced all night. After the music, different members of our team gave testimonies. Then Pastor Dave or a native pastor gave a message.

When altar calls were given, people went forward in droves, especially children and older people. That was so exciting. But one night, I cried out to God, "Where are the teenagers?" Well, the next day we went to a school that had lots of teenagers. Again, the Word was taught and many hands were raised.

The second week, we went to Kampala, the capital of Uganda, where Pastor Dave taught 170 pastors about ministry. They were so hungry and so open. Also, 50 bands throughout Uganda had been invited to a worship seminar that the African and American worship teams led under a tent in a big field. At night, we would go to the other side of the field to host an outdoor crusade with praise and worship and teaching.

One of the most interesting things that happened to me in Africa occurred in Impala. The American team was asked to go forward to pray for the people who responded to the invitation. I went forward then turned and faced the crowd with my eyes closed because I was praying. When I opened my eyes, all I could see was a sea of people coming toward me.

I thought, *Oh, God, how can 12 people possibly minister to this huge group?* Like ocean waves, they flowed past us for about half an hour. We just touched them as they walked by. I cried and cried.

That experience changed my life. I realized then that God can use anyone. He used me because I was a willing vessel. I knew that whatever happened in the people's lives was of God, not of myself. I was only an obedient instrument in God's hands. What a privilege! I would go back in a minute's notice to Africa, but I am willing to go wherever God wants to send me and use me.

Just before we left for Africa, we saw a video about Uganda and learned that the Christians had been praying many, many years, 24 hours a day, for revival. Pastor Dave told us the Ugandans were already praying and experiencing revival before our visit. We just stepped into the middle of whatever God was doing. Only eternity will tell what he did through Freedom Fellowship, by the power of prayer, in the hearts and lives of Ugandans.

I volunteer with Freedom Fellowship because God commands us in Hebrews to remember those in prison as though we are their fellow prisoners. Prison ministry is an act of obedience to God on my part. It is also the love of my life. I talk about Freedom Fellowship everywhere I go and feel privileged to be used by God in prisons in America and around the world.

Chapter 26

My Heart Is in Prison
Mike, Ex-Inmate and Volunteer

In 1988, I moved with my little girl, Carrie, to Cedaredge, Colorado. I also started attending Alcoholics Anonymous at that time. I'd had a drinking and a drug problem since I was 14 years old. I knew I needed to change my lifestyle in order to raise Carrie right.

After six or seven months of progressing through the AA steps, I still felt like things weren't quite right. Something was missing. Although I'd hoped to find an answer in AA, as time went on, I realized it had not filled the emptiness inside of me.

During all those months of AA, Carrie had been attending AWANA Club for boys and girls at the First Baptist Church in Cedaredge. (AWANA is an acronym for Approved Workmen Are Not Ashamed.) One evening in April of 1990, as I drove into the church parking lot to pick up Carrie, the pastor walked out of the church and headed toward my car.

When I rolled down my window, he said, "Your daughter accepted Christ tonight in AWANA Club. Would you like to talk with me about her decision?"

I was out of that car in a flash, like I was compelled to get out. We went into his office and visited a little bit. I told him I'd started studying with the Jehovah Witnesses. He gave me a tract by Billy Graham called "Steps to Peace with God" along with some books about Jehovah Witnesses.

I went right home and read the entire tract while Carrie was getting ready for bed. When I prayed the prayer on the back, I sensed God's Spirit coming inside me. I could feel the emptiness I'd tried to alleviate with alcohol and drugs being filled. The next Sunday, I went to church and haven't looked back at my old life since.

Several of the people in the Cedaredge church were part of Prison Fellowship's ministry in the nearby prisons. I began volunteering with them and soon started a 12-step weekend Bible study for the Delta inmates. It was there I met Donna and other volunteers who came to the prison with her. When they hosted a weekend seminar, I joined them, along with the men in the 12-step group.

In 1996, on Easter Sunday, I was appointed to be a volunteer chaplain at Delta. During the two years I served as chaplain, Freedom Fellowship volunteers visited a couple times a year. That's how I became better acquainted with them. Over the years, as I moved around Colorado, I volunteered with Freedom Fellowship whenever I had an opportunity to do so.

Last fall, I moved to Rawlins, Wyoming, where I've recently started volunteering at the men's penitentiary. I go in every Thursday morning under the auspices of my church to do a Bible study, one-on-one counseling, or whatever is needed.

I've heard that it's hard for a ministry group to get into that particular prison. When I tell people I lead a Bible study at the penitentiary, they're always amazed and ask, "How in the world did you get in there?"

"I prayed," is my simple answer.

My grandson, Michael, and I moved to Rawlins with just our clothes—no furniture. Now we have a house full of furniture that was given to us. I bought a stereo, but it was with money given to me by friends. The only thing I purchased out of my own pocket was a coffee maker.

My refrigerator story is a good one. A couple in the church said to me, "We left a refrigerator at the house where we used to live. You can have it if you want it."

They told me the address and that it was sitting outside the house in the yard. I went to check it out Monday morning before work. It was a nice refrigerator and only about a block from my place. I tried to slide it into my station wagon, but it was too big.

On my way home for lunch, I prayed, "God I know that refrigerator is for me. I need help getting it home. Please keep it there until tonight, when I can ask someone to help me."

As I was eating, God told me to take the doors off the refrigerator. I grabbed my tools, hurried back up the street, and took off the doors. That not only made the refrigerator smaller, it made it lighter, so I could easily tip it and slide it into the back of my car. Then I slid the doors in and drove it to my house. It's a fairly new refrigerator, even has an ice maker.

My heart is in prison ministry and has been since the early '90s. I've taught Sunday school, run the sound board, and preached in church, but no matter what other ministries I do, I always want to go back to prison.

Although I'm a prison volunteer, I have also been incarcerated. I was jailed several times for drinking, plus I did 30 days in a work-release program in Jefferson County,

Colorado. In addition, my father spent a lot of time in the Colorado prison system while I was growing up.

I know what it's like to have a parent in prison, to be in jail myself, and to have a daughter in jail. I've gone in as a volunteer, and I've been a chaplain. I've seen it from all angles. I've been there, done that. I know what works and what doesn't work. That's why I have so much respect for Freedom Fellowship.

When Freedom Fellowship volunteers go to a prison, their desire is to be led by God. They're open to what God wants to do rather than being set on following their own agendas. They're always asked back to the prisons they visit.

The men and women they minister to want them to return, no matter who does the music or who does the teaching. I've seen other people go in with an agenda and not be willing to allow God to take them in a different direction. It doesn't work. The inmates get frustrated.

Another thing I've observed with some prison ministries—if a guy needs experience in preaching, they send him to speak in prison. That's the one place *not* to send a raw recruit. Inmates have time to study the Word. If you mess up, they'll let you know about it. They'll challenge a speaker, unlike people in churches on the outside.

They also challenge each other; however, prison is one place where denominational walls come down. When the residents come together in a chapel service or a seminar, the denominational stuff goes out the window. That's their worship time, and it's precious to them.

On the outside, we fuss about our doctrinal differences. You don't find that in prison. Inmates just believe the Bible. Period. They know who makes the difference in their lives. It's not this denomination or that denomination, not this Bible study or that Bible study. It's not Prison Fellowship or Freedom Fellowship. It's not the chaplain. It's Jesus.

He's the one who changes lives using ordinary people and his Word to deliver his message of salvation, love and forgiveness behind bars.

Chapter 27

On the Other Side
Christine and John, Ex-Inmates

Getting married in 1999 was just one of God's many miracles in our lives. Long before our wedding, we were both incarcerated at Larimer County Detention Center and knew of each other but had no idea we'd someday be married. It was all God's timing, his perfect timing.

We met again when we were both on parole. We weren't supposed to hang out with other ex-inmates, but we met at church, and the Lord just let it all fall into place. We even had the same parole officer.

Since we had to get permission from our parole officer to get married, Donna talked with him for us. He could see we were good for each other, that we helped each other through the rough times. He was also a new Christian who was learning to be in tune with the ways God works.

(John)

My brothers and I grew up with a bad alcoholic as our stepdad. He hit my mom all the time and did cruel things to punish us, like forcing us to jump on our knees on the gravel outside. My mom did the best she could to help us. Still, it was rough growing up without a real father, feeling jealous of others who had one.

We never talked about God at our house, but we sometimes went to church on weekends. My grandmother had a big, gold Bible at her house we weren't allowed to touch. I was curious about it, but I never opened it or read it. Christianity was a mystery to me.

Thanks to Freedom Fellowship's ministry at LCDC, as an adult I began to realize how easy it is to know the Lord, how simple it is to accept Jesus into your heart. I became a Christian at LCDC and gave my life to God. I went to all the Bible studies and really got into God during the 10 months I was incarcerated in Fort Collins. When it came time go to prison, I was kind of scared, but not really, because I had the Lord in me.

Prison was okay. I just stuck with being a Christian. My time behind bars gave me a chance to study the Bible for hours at a time. I even got baptized there.

The Lord had to put me in a place where he could talk to me. Some people are so stubborn they don't listen. I was glad God snatched me up and sent me to prison; otherwise, I'd be dead.

I played in the chapel band. We had a good time, got the chapel rocking. People said we glowed when we were playing and singing. We just tried to be fishermen for Jesus and lead people to God.

It's not any easier to live for the Lord in prison than on the outside, but you have more focus, because you're not distracted with all that happens on the outside. Many prisoners have beautiful relationships with God. I don't want to go back to prison; however, I'd love to have all that time to focus on spiritual things.

Actually, one of my goals is to return to prison. When I left, I said, "I'll be back, but next time I'll come back on the other side." I'd like to share my testimony in prisons and take in bands to play worship music.

I'd also like to organize Christian concerts and passion plays and events that get the attention of younger kids. I have several children of my own and really love kids. I want to help them learn about Jesus at an early age, so they don't get into trouble like I did.

I'd also like to have an intervention ministry to help people just getting out of jail keep their focus. The more focused I am, the better I can help someone else stay focused. No one can do it on his or her own.

(Christine)

My earliest memory of Jesus is from Bible pictures of him reading stories to little children. For a long time, I thought he was a guy who read stories to kids. That's about all I knew about God, even though I went to church.

During my growing up years, I tried to be the best kid possible. At about 17 or 18, however, I got bored with being good. I started drinking and hanging out with the wrong people, doing the gang thing. We didn't call it a gang back then—it was just a group of us who drank together. When we drank, we had to find something exciting to do, which usually involved trouble.

I didn't do drugs. Alcohol was enough to get me into trouble. Eventually, I ended up in jail. The first time I was in for two months. Then I was out for three months but got into trouble again.

I was sent back to LCDC for nine months. That's when Donna started counseling me. I rededicated my life to the Lord and was baptized in jail. I really got into my Bible, learning a lot through mail-in Bible studies.

Donna has been there every step of the way for me. All through LCDC, she helped out. She visited me and brought me special Bible verses. The verses always spoke to my situation. Whatever I was thinking about, the Lord gave her just the right verses for me.

She'd read the verse then ask, "How does that apply to your life right now?" I'd know exactly what the Lord was telling me. I think that is one of the most awesome things she does for prisoners.

I went to church every day in the county jail, sometimes three times a day. We started a prayer circle. We weren't supposed to touch each other, but the guards allowed us to hold hands in the prayer circle. It was cool. I was able to help a lot of people who were going to be in jail for a long time. I helped them focus.

I thank God for sending me to jail. That's kind of weird to say, but I hate to think where I'd be now if he hadn't interrupted my drinking and partying. I was a stubborn kid who had to be taken to the bottom to see the right way.

When I got out of jail, I went to the Freedom Fellowship support group every week and to church every week. I did really good for a while. Then I quit going to church and quit going to the support group and ended up in jail again for two months.

After that, I was sent to prison for a year. Prison wasn't really all that bad. The worst part was not being with my kids or other family members. I worked for a landscaper while I was incarcerated. He had me draw landscape designs. That was fun, and it kept me occupied.

The church in prison was awesome. It was just so cool. We had Bible studies and prayer groups every morning. Five or six of us prayed together for an hour before we went to work.

When I was in prison, I had so much time for just me and God. I think the Spirit of God is everywhere, but I was so much more in tune in prison. I was listening to the Lord more and reading my Bible more.

We definitely prayed more, because we had lots of time. I don't know what it is about prison walls, but they seem to hold more of the Spirit. You can feel the Spirit out here, but there's something special in jail.

I love going to schools to talk with the kids about what God has done in my life. I grew up in Fort Collins, and I was into the whole gang thing, all the stuff that kids today think is cool. Some of them recognize me because I used to party with their older brothers and sisters. When they hear me talking about where I'm at now, they think, *That's the girl who used to drink with my brother.* It's an awesome privilege to share my testimony with teenagers.

I remember the morning we were scheduled to speak at Frontier High School, an alternative school for kids who've gotten into trouble. I prayed, "Okay, Lord, I know the one question that's going to be on their minds. They're going to ask me about gang loyalty. What do I say when someone asks me about my gang and how we always said, 'South Side 'til I die'?"

After I prayed, the thought was put into my head, *When you accepted God, you died to that former life, that old lifestyle, and became a new person. Now you're alive in him.*

As I explained that concept to those kids, I could see on their faces they had that question in their minds. God gave me the answer I needed for them that day.

Another time, I was scheduled to talk to first and second graders. I didn't know what to say. I prayed, "Please, Lord, give me the words to speak." I don't like talking in front of people. It makes me nervous. But as soon as I got up there, I felt comfortable and couldn't keep quiet. God gave me the words I needed.

I especially like to talk to children. I pray something I say will keep them from going through the same stuff I went through. I want them to know how awesome God is and how he can guide their entire lives.

Chapter 28

God Opened My Heart
Richard, Ex-Inmate

When I was two years old, my mom and I moved from Michigan to Jackson, Wyoming, to live with my grandpa on his horse ranch. In the third grade, I started attending a boarding school near my dad back in Michigan. But I still spent summers in Wyoming.

And every summer from age 13 on, I competed in rodeos. I was into all kinds of sports, from football to track to swimming—everything but hockey. I even received a swimming scholarship to the University of Michigan. Playing sports was pretty much my life; it kept me out of trouble. I didn't drink, didn't smoke, didn't do drugs. Never gave my parents much to worry about.

At the University of Michigan, I studied outdoor education and business for two years. Then I joined the Army, which had been my goal all through high school. In the four years I was in the Army, I finished my business degree and got married, although that marriage didn't last long.

After the Army, I went to truck-driving school then drove for North American Van Lines for eight or nine months. I missed the military, so I talked with the local Navy recruiter. When he found out about my swimming background, he offered to send me to SCUBA school. That convinced me to join the Navy, and I soon found myself at diving school in Pensacola, Florida.

While I was there, my superiors discovered I was a country boy who could hunt, so they asked me if I wanted to go to sniper school. I jumped at the opportunity and was transferred to Virginia to learn how to be a sniper.

Sniper training is no fun—just a lot of work and a lot of emotional detachment. You have to completely remove yourself from who you are. For the most part, it fit my persona. Although I'd always been very involved in team sports, I was a loner. I could lose myself in whatever I was doing. I'm still that way to some degree.

From sniper school, I was sent to demolition school because of my swimming background and SCUBA training as well as my mathematical abilities. Finally, I was assigned to a unit at Coronado Island, San Diego, California.

My spotter and I spent time in the Middle East, in China, in Russia, and many other locations. We got around. I was home maybe 85 days each year. We were always going somewhere. I was an urban sniper. We'd parachute into the outskirts of a city, sneak into town at night, then sit on a rooftop for days and days waiting for the right moment to fulfill our mission.

Then came the Desert Storm conflict. I went in on the USS Kennedy, the first ship in. We were in the Straits of Hormuz for three weeks clearing mines so the rest of the ships could get in. When we left Desert Storm, we had to clear mines again. One exploded close to me and my partner, and we sustained some pretty severe steam burns from it. I received a purple heart for that one and a bronze star for pulling my partner out of the water. He was closer to the blast than I was.

After my recovery, I was sent to Somalia. While there, I was assigned as a sniper to the search-and rescue-team that went in after the downed helicopter depicted in the movie "Black Hawk Down." I spent 120 hours on rooftops on that mission.

My military career ended on a Somalian rooftop, when I was shot with a little .25 caliber bullet by a woman who was at least 70-years old. She just snuck up on us and shot me. I'm not sure why, but I think she was upset we were disturbing her birds.

I received another purple heart for being injured, plus a silver star for valor. But the Somalian incident ended my military career. I lost my spleen, part of my colon, and part of my stomach. I had to have a lot of surgery. I loved the military and didn't want to leave the Navy, although I have to admit the sniper thing was starting to wear on my conscience.

I was discharged from the Navy in December of 1992. By that time, I had married again. We moved to Jackson, where I was a river guide, a fishing guide, a hunting guide—you name it, anything outdoors. That's what Jackson is all about.

From there, we relocated to Arizona, where we were part owners of a restaurant. I also helped a rancher during calving season. The guy I rode herd with carried a Bible in his saddlebag. Every time he got a chance, he'd whip out his Bible and start reading.

I was a smart mouth back then and gave him a hard time. He maintained his composure, though I became both frustrated and curious. Finally, I started asking him questions about the Bible, and he answered them.

After a couple weeks of talking and reading and having horseback Bible study, he asked if I'd like to have Jesus in my life. I said, "Yes."

So we climbed off our horses, and right there in the middle of an Arizona cow pasture, surrounded by a herd of longhorn cattle, I got down on my knees and asked Jesus into my heart. I cried and cried, for the first time in a long, long time.

My wife and I lived in Arizona for almost two years, but neither of us could take the heat, so we moved to Estes Park, Colorado. In Estes, I forgot all about my new relationship with Jesus and started drinking and partying. I turned into a hellion—I was not a nice guy.

My behavior affected our marriage. Right when things hit rock bottom between my wife and me, we found out we were pregnant. Despite that good news, things fell apart between us, and my life went downhill fast.

That's when my felony charge came up. I was managing a fast-food restaurant at the time and took money out of the deposits to pay the mortgage payment on a house we'd just purchased. The authorities took a long time to investigate the theft. Eventually, I spent a couple weeks at the Larimer County Detention Center and was given a deferred sentence. But it wasn't long before I violated the deferred sentence by missing a class I was supposed to go to. The judge revoked the deferred sentence and put me on probation.

After our son was born, we lost the house and moved into an apartment. Then we got a call from a lawyer telling us we had a house in Cheyenne that had been left to me by my mom, whose great uncle had left it to her. The timing was perfect, a God thing, even if we didn't realize it. We gladly moved to Cheyenne and into the house. The state of Colorado transferred my probation to Wyoming.

At first, things were good for us in Cheyenne, although we had some difficulties because I worked too much. I managed an Arby's, worked as a bartender and a bouncer at night, helped a farmer with his cows, and worked part-time doing sales. When I wasn't working, I was at the bar.

On Saint Patrick's Day, 1999, I did a 16-hour day at the restaurant. Then I was asked to tend bar that night. When I closed the place down at three o'clock in the morning, I was bone tired. I drank my shift drink—one beer, which I didn't even finish—and locked up.

As I drove out of the parking lot, I was so tired I drove over the curb. A Laramie County sheriff's officer sitting across the street saw what happened and pulled me over. He cited me for "driving while ability impaired." Because of that citation, I violated my probation, which brought me back to Fort Collins and LCDC in June of 1999.

As a newcomer to the jail, I observed Donna talking with some guys in the pod. I didn't have any idea who she was, but she had this light around her. She just had this glow. One day she came in to talk to someone who was gone, so I asked to talk with her, not about anything in particular. I just wanted to have somebody to talk to. I didn't know anybody in Fort Collins at that time.

I was not aware Donna was the detention center chaplain. I didn't know anything about her. We went into a room and visited, and she led me back to God. After that visit, Donna and I talked and talked about the Lord. She came to see me twice a week while I was in Larimer County.

I was sentenced to the Halfway House and did four-and-a-half months there before I went out on non-resident status. I moved into a trailer house, worked at the International House of Pancakes, went to the required meetings, and did everything right.

Then some money came up missing from IHOP. I got blamed because, although I was on vacation the day it disappeared, I'd gone in to check the schedule. The next day, my first day back at work, my case manager plus someone from IHOP and someone from the Halfway House, came and took me away from work.

They drove to my home, searched my place, and found a beer bottle beside the porch. It wasn't my bottle, but they asked if I'd had a drink. I'd been out beside a lake the night before talking to God because my wife had just filed for a divorce. I consumed part of a beer that night, so I admitted it. They took me to jail, where I stayed for three or four weeks.

Then they sent me back into the Halfway House to do the six-month program there. After six months, I was put back on non-resident again. I started working at vacuum cleaner and sewing machine shop, doing sales and service.

One evening after a tough week, I looked at the two paychecks sitting on the coffee table and thought, *I really, really want a drink*. But I knew the consequences of drinking, so I decided to open up a bank account and deposit the checks. That way I wouldn't be tempted. It would require too many steps to go get a drink.

The next day, I had a meeting with my case manager. She asked me where my cash was.

I said, "It's in the bank."

She didn't like that. I'd forgotten it's against the Community Corrections rules to have a savings or checking account or credit cards. I was thrown into jail again, and the plan was to send me back to the Halfway House for eight months. I said, "No way. Forget it. I'm tired of you people. I've been through almost three years of this. I'm sick of it."

So they sent me to prison. That was my alternative. I was there for 172 days from the time I left until the time I came home. It was definitely better than the Halfway House.

I'm on parole right now, catching up with my life. Without Freedom Fellowship, I wouldn't be where I am now. I can absolutely state that as a fact—no ifs, ands or buts about it.

Chapter 29

New Creations in Christ
Ginny, Board of Directors

I probably never would have volunteered in jails and prisons if my husband hadn't died in 1976. I had three teenagers to clothe and feed, so I went to nursing school for an LPN degree. After I graduated, I found a job at the hospital and worked there for several years. Then I heard about an LPN opening at the local jail. Something told me I should apply, that the position would be more than pushing pills.

Though I was hired, within five months I was fired for taking one of the inmates into my home after he was released from the jail. At that time, there was no rule against fraternizing with ex-inmates, so the sheriff lied about why he fired me. It was plastered all over the newspapers that I was let go because I was an incompetent nurse. But the nursing supervisor at Poudre Valley Hospital knew that story wasn't true. She rehired me and I went back to work at the hospital. I also continued to open my home to ex-inmates for several years.

I don't remember exactly how or when I started going into the prisons, but I do remember the first time I went with Prison Fellowship to the Wyoming State Penitentiary in Rawlins. That's when I met Donna Roth. She'd just started Freedom Fellowship but was still taking people into prisons through Prison Fellowship seminars.

It was slow going at first for Freedom Fellowship. I think we only did five seminars the first year. In 2002, we offered 46 prison seminars in Colorado and Wyoming, plus Bible studies, church services, baptisms, mental health classes, and counseling at the Larimer County Detention Center, We also provided an ex-inmate support group and started an adult church for sex-offenders.

In the beginning stages, the local jail ministry consisted of just one church service held on a Sunday evening. Now Donna is the detention center chaplain. Freedom Fellowship has grown more and more every year.

I've been a board member and the ministry's administrative assistant for around 11 years. I answer the phone, set up seminars, send out schedules of events, board meetings, prayer meetings, support groups, seminars and training classes, keep track of our volunteers, make sure the volunteers get the required background checks and training, and edit and type Donna's correspondence.

I go to a prison about once a month as part of a Freedom Fellowship team and help where needed for that particular seminar. In the past, I worked with the support group. Sometimes I provided transportation to the meetings, and sometimes I acted as somewhat of a chaperone for the group. We like to have the inmates lead the meetings, but we also have a host volunteer there to provide direction and encouragement, and to keep things orderly. The support group is effective, particularly when the ex-inmates lead it.

For those interested in volunteering with Freedom Fellowship, we need people who can teach or lead praise-and-worship music, which the inmates really enjoy. We also need volunteers to take care of the refreshments, the books, the book drawings and completion certificates, and to run the overhead projector. Support people who mingle with and minister to the inmates plus help keep things organized are just as important as those who speak and lead music.

In addition to prison and jail volunteers, we have plenty of service opportunities around town. Area churches collect used books and packaged cookies for us to take into the prisons. We need people who'll give a few hours a month to pick up the cookies and books and sort the books.

There are also times when we could use assistance in finding housing, transportation, employment, and food and clothing for needy individuals or families. We also need financial contributions. Most of all, we need prayer warriors who will support Freedom Fellowship with daily prayer.

Being a part of Freedom Fellowship from the beginning has been a real blessing for me. It's a constant thrill to see people once labeled "incorrigible" become new creations in Christ and assets to society rather than liabilities.

Chapter 30

Uganda Diary Highlights
Chaplain Donna Roth, Founder and Director

Tuesday, July 31

Today we went to a prison in Itoro. Eight hundred inmates—men and women—came to the service. Many received Christ.

The conditions at that prison are very bad. The inmates are not given clothing, hygiene supplies or medicine, and many are sick. The only clothing they have is what they had on when they were arrested or what someone may have brought them from the outside. They break twigs off the trees to clean their teeth, so they were happy to receive the toothbrushes we gave them.

I told them my K-Mart story about how God miraculously gave me medicine, and they understood it. One inmate told me he and many others are very sick and cannot get medicine. I encouraged him to believe God as I did, because God would provide. The Lord impressed on me that we should start sending money for soap, toothpaste, clothing and medicine.

We visited another prison with a population of 2,000. Those inmates also suffer from AIDS, malaria, typhoid, tuberculosis and other diseases, which are not medically treated. I was told that a prisoner sentenced to more than a year will most likely die before his or her sentence is up. With that many inmates, I only saw four visitors bring in food and clothing while we were there.

Wednesday, August 1

The crusade started in Iganga last evening. About 15,000 people came out. The big field was filled with all ages of people, from infants to elderly people. We were able to pray with many to receive Christ and also to receive the Holy Spirit. Many of the people who came were very sick. Malaria and AIDS are prevalent here. One family I talked with had no food.

Thursday, August 2

The local church pastors conference started in Iganga today. I taught about Holy Spirit baptism and shared stories of God's miracles in my life.

David shared his testimony and preached. Mike also preached. At the end of the service, I was privileged to pray for 12 African pastors to receive the baptism of the Holy Spirit. I also prayed for a baby who had worms. I sensed she was immediately healed because she stopped crying when we finished praying.

An African invited me to go with him into a thatched hut. He told me some people in there wanted to be saved. My journalist friend assured me it was okay to go in. Inside, I saw a big pot in the middle of the room and people sitting around it sipping something out of the pot with very long straws.

I asked my friend, "What is this?" She told me we were in a bar.

The crusades continued tonight. People were delivered from demons and healed of malaria, AIDS and other diseases. Many were saved.

Friday, August 3

We visited a school today, grades one through 12. My grandson, Scott, shared his testimony. I was so proud of him. He told the students that it took him a long time to save the money to make this trip, but he was so glad he did.

He said, "We Americans may have more money than you, but you are the richer ones because you are such loving people."

He gave a tribute to me and thanked me for seeing to it that he was raised as a Christian. He also told them Jesus died on the cross for them as well as for him.

Monday, August 6

The Kampala crusade began this evening. Again, there were many salvations and healings. Many individuals were delivered from demons and came forward to put their witchcraft symbols up on the stage.

Tuesday, August 7

We went into another prison today in the Lweza District. Both men and women attended the service. Many of the women had babies or small children with them. Edith, Kris and I were all able to share our testimonies. Seventy-five inmates received the Lord as their Savior, and many received the baptism of the Holy Spirit.

Wednesday, August 8

Today we went to a medium-security prison for men and women. An ex-inmate joined us and told the prisoners how God had miraculously released her from prison. I was able to pray for 350 men at the men's prison for salvation, healing, and the baptism of the Holy Spirit.

We tried to get into a high security prison, but prior arrangements had not been made, so the guards wouldn't let us in. Sometimes African volunteers don't understand they can't just show up when they feel like it at a prison, the way they do other places.

Thursday, August 9

I spoke about prison ministry at the pastors' conference today. Pastors from Uganda, Tanzania, Mali and Rwanda attended. They all asked us to come to their churches and share about prison ministry. Three pastors said they want to start Freedom Fellowship chapters in their churches. We were even asked to stay another week and go to other countries to share our work.

Afterthoughts

We learned to accept many cultural differences and inconveniences while in Uganda. We could only drink bottled water. Few places had running water, so we didn't get a lot of showers. The ones we did get were cold. Very few flush toilets were available. Most of the homes had holes in the ground outside the houses for toilets.

A few months ago, a Freedom Fellowship chapter was started in Uganda. It's already going strong. In the first two weeks, the two men heading up the ministry visited nine prisons and led 357 inmates to the Lord.

Since then, they've gained other team members and gone into prisons where the Gospel has never before been shared. Many inmates are being saved through their work. The Colorado Freedom Fellowship group is sending financial assistance, as we promised. We've been invited to return to Uganda and to also go to Tanzania.

After returning home, I heard from an African pastor from Rwanda who's interested in prison ministry. He'd like to collaborate with Freedom Fellowship. He told me there are one-million political prisoners in Rwanda as a result of the recent civil war. These prisoners will never be released, and no one is allowed to visit them. If a friend or relative did attempt a visit, they'd be considered a traitor to the present regime and end up in prison, too. We covet your prayers for guidance as we organize a Freedom Fellowship chapter in Rwanda.

When I first became a Christian, I prayed, "Lord, please don't send me to Africa as a missionary." I'm so glad he ignored my request. I'm amazed at the love he's placed in my heart for the African people, especially the inmates.

Chapter 31

It Just Keeps Getting Better
Ron, Ex-Inmate

I grew up in a small New Mexico town about as big as the Colorado State University campus. Wasn't much to do there. I hung around with the tough guys and wanted to be like them, so I started drinking alcohol at a young age. It's a wonder I didn't kill somebody or get killed myself while driving drunk. One time, I blacked out in my car on train tracks, and it was hit by a train. The impact spun the car around, but I wasn't hurt.

Back then, I didn't acknowledge God. I knew my mom was praying for me, so I thought I didn't need to worry, despite the fact I was a really, really bad person. I was wretched. I had to do it all myself.

Donna Roth led me to the Lord at the Larimer County Detention Center. When I accepted Jesus Christ as my Lord and Savior and completely surrendered to him, it felt like a burden was lifted off my back. I felt peace and freedom in my heart. After 15 years, the void in my soul—the hole in my heart—was finally filled.

I was later baptized in the Holy Spirit and baptized with water. I started reading the Word, praying and acknowledging God in everything I did. I attended a really good Bible study Freedom Fellowship hosted at the jail.

As soon as I moved into the Halfway House, God blessed me with a job at CSU. I got out of jail on the 13th of

September and was employed on the 14th. It's amazing what God can do when you allow him to work in your life.

I knew I had to continue my walk with the Lord. If I didn't, I was going to fail again. I started going to the Freedom Fellowship support group that meets on Wednesday evenings. Recently, I was asked to be the group leader, which means I lead the group in prayer and Bible study. Then we share what's going on in our lives. We pray for each other and always have a good time of fellowship.

I believe my purpose in life is to lead and teach inmates and ex-inmates. God can draw them with his Spirit just like he did me. I tell other ex-felons what God has done for me and encourage them to go to the support group. If I had had a support group the first time I got out of jail, I don't think I would have relapsed.

I attend a prayer meeting on Monday nights. On Tuesday nights, I go to a "Strategies for Self-Improvement" class at Community Corrections. I also attend another class called "Road to Freedom," which is similar to AA but more like mental health therapy. It's scripturally based and is about getting your life in balance. It teaches you how to react to stress and emotions.

God wants us to live life abundantly in all areas—finances, health, fellowship with Christians, communication with our families, and helping those in need. Instead of living a negative life and complaining about everything, God says to be content with what we have and depend on him for our needs. It's very simple, but we make it complicated because we want to do it our way.

I used to be proud. I didn't need anybody's help, even though I was headed down destruction road like a freight train without brakes. Before, if I saw people in trouble, I'd help them for money. I had a four-wheel drive truck. When I saw someone stuck in mud or snow, I'd say, "For 20 bucks, I'll pull you out." Now I live to help other people and be of service to them.

The thought of a drink is repulsive to me since I became a Christian. That's not my doing; it's the Spirit of God. I used to drink and do drugs constantly. I was evil to the max. Today, by the grace and mercy of God and his faithfulness, I'm free from addiction.

The other day, as I was standing on the street corner waiting for a ride, I looked down. There sat a full bottle of whiskey. I knew the devil had someone put it there to tempt me. I said, "Get behind me, Satan!" It didn't even bother me.

My family is amazed by the change in me. I used to be irritable, never really a part of my family. I was always too busy running around with my construction friends, chasing drugs and alcohol. I was never home. Before, my mouth spewed profanity, one swear word after another. Now, I just want to express what the Lord has done for me and share the love from him I feel in my heart. Only because of his unlimited love am I here. All my family talks about is the difference God has made in my life.

It hasn't been easy for me to change my attitudes, my way of thinking. I was set in my ways. The hardest thing was to forgive myself. I knew God had forgiven me and delivered me from addiction. But it took a long time to forgive myself. However, once I did, I took off. Even my case manager and the people at the Halfway House noticed.

Prayer brought me to that point. Down in my heart, I knew God would forgive me. He said, *Why do you carry that garbage around? Give it to me. Whatever burdens and guilt you have, whatever hurts, I'll take them away and never bring them back. Forgive yourself.*

Every morning before I go to work, I ask the Lord to bless me for that day and only for that day. The Bible tells us not to worry about tomorrow, because today has enough worries of its own. As long as I pray in the morning and ask the Lord to direct me, I can handle whatever happens at work. When you learn to live by the voice of God, it gets louder and louder. I'm not saying I'm Superman. By the end of the day I'm exhausted, but when I ask the Lord for the strength to endure and to continue, the strength is automatic, supernatural.

One day, I went outside on break, looked up at the sky and thought, *Our God is so awesome.* Just then, God poured out his Spirit on me for I don't know how long. It seemed like a long time. I felt his presence all around, inside and out, and a tingling sensation all over my body. I felt a flow of heat, like when you're cold and you go inside the house to bundle up in a nice warm blanket. I felt content and comforted, warm, secure and safe. From the inside out, the sensation flowed, while I praised God.

I never used to pray a lot, but the more I pray, the easier it is for me to communicate with God. He keeps opening my ears to hear him and my heart to receive. I pray every day, "God, broaden my coasts." Then I watch for opportunities to help people. Like Donna says, it's so fulfilling to do God's work.

Even though I live in my own place now, I pray for Community Corrections every morning when I have my quiet time with the Lord. I pray for Larimer County Detention

Center. I pray for my brothers and sisters in jails and prisons. I pray for the prison ministries. I pray for my family. I ask God to help anybody I can think of who needs prayer.

A friend I knew on the streets moved into the Halfway House about a week before I left. He wanted to tell war stories like we used to when we smoked and drank and ran around together. I said, "Sam, I don't do that anymore."

He told me about some guy being a child molester. I said, "Why don't we pray for him?"

Sam said, "When did all this happen, all this prayer and religious stuff?"

I said, "Sam, I'm not the same person I used to be. I have a love and a passion for people now. I don't manipulate, steal, cheat, lie or any of that stuff anymore. I try to help people and lead them to the Lord."

Several people at the Halfway House asked me to pray for them. They saw the joy I had in my heart. The Lord was shining through me.

His Spirit continues to work through me to reach people for salvation, for his glory. What God has done in my life never ceases to amaze me. Day by day, it just keeps getting better.

Chapter 32

Hooray, Colorado
Helain, Board of Directors

I became interested in prison ministry when I read Chuck Colson's book "Born Again." When I later learned of Prison Fellowship's work at the jail in Fort Collins, I spoke with some of the volunteers, who suggested I talk with Donna Roth. At that time, Donna was with Prison Fellowship, but the Lord had laid it on her heart to start another jail and prison ministry.

After Freedom Fellowship became a reality, I joined the group as a volunteer and as a board member. I was learning to play the guitar back then and eventually became proficient enough to play in public. I led the singing for the jail services on a weekly basis for years.

Nowadays, I only attend the jail services once a month, because I go to more prison seminars than I used to. I was single when I started with Freedom Fellowship. One year later, I married Kevin. He prefers the prison ministry, so we do that together. We participate in four-to-five seminars a year, and I usually lead praise and worship.

In the beginning, a large group of volunteers led the music, almost like a band. As we scheduled more and more seminars, we were stretched thinner and thinner. Now, I lead the music by myself most of the time. At prisons where inmates have bands or play instruments, I ask them to help me. It's wonderful when such great musicians back me up.

I recently started teaching at some of the seminars. We team teach, which gives the teachers a break. Plus, the inmates seem to enjoy the variety. Kevin does fitness training for a living and has competed in many power-lifting competitions over the years. He's even set records. Sometimes, he takes videos of his competitions to Freedom Fellowship seminars. After giving his testimony and reading several Scriptures, he shows a video. A lot of inmates are really into power lifting, so they enjoy watching the competition and talking with him.

I was the treasurer for Freedom Fellowship for the first five years as we set up the financial structure. Now, I edit the ministry newsletter, "Free Indeed," and serve on the board of directors. The newsletters go to the jail and the prisons and to some of the local churches that support us. Most of our copies are taken to the prisons, so we like to use articles and stories that inmates are interested in reading. They seem to really appreciate them.

Although my traveling time has been limited by my work schedule, I've been on some exciting trips with Freedom Fellowship. One year, we went to a military prison in Leavenworth, Kansas, which was an exhilarating experience. We also held a seminar at a Texas prison where some Colorado inmates were incarcerated. That was the most exciting seminar I've attended.

The Colorado inmates were housed in a very old jail that still had bars on the cells. When we entered, we walked down a long hallway with cells along each side. Men waved through the bars and shouted, "Hooray, Colorado!" They were so glad to see us. The whole first floor came to the seminar. We had standing room only. What an awesome response to our visit and ministry.

It was a long trip, but a real blessing. We always return from seminars on a spiritual high, talking all the way home about the awesome things God has done. We are ministered to more than we minister.

Freedom Fellowship has been a springboard for our volunteers to become involved in other ministries. Randy is now a missionary in Mexico. Debbie is the director of an international ministry that supports Jewish people who want to return to Israel. Rodney is attending a music school in Mexico to learn to lead praise and worship in Spanish. One of the men who used to teach our seminars moved to Texas to go to Bible school.

Freedom Fellowship has a core group of people who have a heart for the ministry and who've become good friends. It's a great place for friendship and fellowship. Everyone needs a small group. We also meet a lot of interesting people through Freedom Fellowship—prisoners, volunteers, chaplains, guards, and other staff members—neat, neat people. Some of the inmates have been coming to our seminars since we started. That's a treat for us because we've known them for years and years now.

They may get transferred to another prison, but they're still in the Colorado system, and they know us when we come. It's always a thrill to see them again, and even more of a thrill to see them get out of prison and live for the Lord.

Chapter 33

I'm Not Going to Prison
Gary, Ex-Inmate

I was raised in a Christian home but started hanging out with the wrong people and getting into trouble even as a kid. I was very rebellious, and it hurts me to remember the things I did to my family. I believe it was my mother's prayers that brought me back. She prayed and prayed and prayed for me, and God answered her prayers.

I was 10-years old and in the fourth grade the first time I smoked marijuana. When I was 14 or 15, I started using alcohol socially. At 16, my social drinking became a habit when I got a job at a pizza place where they sold beer. The manager was a senior in high school and a partier. Every night after we closed the doors, we drank beer while we cleaned the place.

After I graduated from high school, I studied auto body repair at Wyoming Technical Institute in Laramie, Wyoming. For me, it was one drunken-high party the whole time I was there. I got into trouble a couple of times, but my punishment was just a slap on the hand. I'd pay a fine and be done with the problem.

Following school, I returned to Colorado, got married, and had kids. At age 28, I lost my first marriage due to alcohol and drugs. That's when my problems really started. I'd get drunker than drunk and do crazy things, like drive as fast as I could around Horsetooth Lake on my way home from the bar.

I started getting into more serious trouble with the law. I got a DUI, then sold my house and spent all the profit on cocaine and women within two months. I was caught driving without a license two or three times. Then I got another DUI. But the system kept giving me chances. They even put me through alcohol classes. After class, however, the students would all walk across the street to the bar together.

I kept getting into trouble and eventually spent a month in the Larimer County Detention Center, which kind of woke me up. But I still wasn't ready to change. I got out, got in trouble again, and went back into work release. I went through just about every program the county offers—work release, weekenders, straight time. Then I was given "habitual offender status," which meant that the next time I was caught, it would be considered a felony.

Well, one morning my ex-wife called me at work to tell me our daughter was sick at school. She was frantic because her car was broken and she had no way to get our daughter home.

I jumped into a car from work and headed for the school, but I got busted because I didn't slow down for road construction. It was a God move, although I didn't realize it at the time. My arrest made me bitter. I was just trying to help my daughter.

So I got my first felony. But I thought, *I can beat this. I'll get a good lawyer.* I spent $3,000 on a lawyer, and he got me a good deal. They gave me another month in jail plus a year's intensive probation, where I had to check in all the time, go to classes twice a week, and be constantly monitored. I attended the classes and quit drugs for a while but soon started using again.

Thinking I could beat the system, I drank goldenseal and other herbal teas I'd heard would give a false urine analysis. I even drank vinegar, thinking I was fooling the system, thinking I was so cool. I did six UAs without an apparent problem.

After the seventh one, the teacher said, "I need to talk with you after class."

I said, in my most cool way, "What's up?"

"Your first six UAs were hot for THC and marijuana and this last one for THC and cocaine. I'm going to have to drop you from the program and do a motion to revoke your probation."

I thought, *I'm not going to prison!* and ran to Loveland, where I hid out at a guy's shop. I didn't want the authorities or my ex-wife to find me, since I didn't pay child support. I was a deadbeat dad. I was a deadbeat everything.

I worked for several months for the guy who owned the shop. He also sold drugs on the side. I'd work all week for him and still end up owing him money for my usage. It was awful. There were times when my heart was pounding so hard from the cocaine I thought I was having a heart attack. I'd pray, "God, please. If you're really there, you need to help me. I can't help myself."

One night I was driving to another guy's house to pick up an ounce of cocaine. On my way through town, I noticed the dash lights go out in the car, which meant the tail lights were also out. A cop in Loveland signaled for me to pull over, and I did. But, when he got out of his car to walk up to mine, I put my car into gear and took off.

I started the chase, yet I was scared to death. My adrenaline was pumping so hard and my heart was pounding so fast I could barely breathe. More and more police vehicles joined our high-speed race through town. I remember a blur of flashing lights, sirens and crazy driving—running cars off the road, going through stoplights, bouncing off curbs. I was lucky I didn't kill somebody, including myself.

By the time I was halfway to Fort Collins, so many cops were chasing me I decided to bail. As I turned a corner, I opened the car door and flew out. After a tuck and a roll, I was up running. (Obviously, I'd seen too many cop shows.) My car crashed into someone's house, and I was captured within minutes.

About a week later, I was released on bond. While I was in Loveland waiting to go to court and at the end of my rope, the pastor from the church I grew up in showed up at my hideout. I was frightened but glad to see him.

He told me the Lord sent him to me. Then he asked if I wanted Christ in my life. I said I did. He prayed with me, and the Holy Spirit just knocked me down. I sobbed and sobbed.

The system gave me another chance. This time, they put me into a community corrections program. I spent four months in jail waiting to get a bed in the Halfway House. That's when I got to know Donna and other Freedom Fellowship volunteers. I saw the love and the peace and the joy they had.

I went through the Halfway House program with flying colors. I had no write-ups and was in and out in record time. I was able to stay away from drugs when I got out, but Satan knew my other weakness—women. He put one in my life who professed to be a Christian, despite the fact she smoked pot and drank a lot.

I was around the booze and the pot for months without any problems. Then we started having troubles in our relationship. On top of that, I saw my ex-wife and my kids during the holidays. That was painful for me. One night after Christmas, I got loaded, drank myself into a blackout, and drove without a license.

When I woke up the next day in my own bed, I had blood all over me. I must have gotten into a fight and didn't even know it. When I looked out the window, I couldn't see my car, so I rode my bike around the neighborhood looking for it. I found it four or five blocks away. That scared me, so I called my case manager.

Since it was a Saturday, I left a message on his machine saying I'd used again, and I was scared. "I want to take care of this," I said. "I want help." A week or so later, he contacted me and told me to turn myself in to the Halfway House, which I did.

I thought they'd send me to a treatment program, like they had countless other people who used. That's what I wanted. But I was told, "We've revoked you from our program."

I said, "You're not going to send me to treatment?"

They said, "Sure we are—prison. You'll learn there."

I didn't understand that. I felt bitter because it wasn't equal justice. Plus, I had to sit in the county jail a couple more months waiting to go to prison. I told Donna, "That's what I get for being honest. I should have lied, never said anything. They would have never known."

Donna said, "But you know what happened, and God knows what happened. God also knows where your heart is. You've turned yourself in, and he's going to respect that." She helped me get over my bitterness. That's when I decided to give everything, not just part of my life, to God.

My ex-wife brought my oldest daughter in to see me at LCDC. I was happy and smiling. She said, "Dad, why are you so happy? You're in jail!"

"I'm freer now than I've ever been in my life," I told her. "I might be behind bars, but I'm free."

Standard procedure when a person first goes to prison is to be locked down for 23 hours a day. I was allowed out for one hour to take a shower and use a telephone. I had a Bible with me that I read and read and read. I also did calisthenics to keep fit. The isolation was hard, but it was good for me. It gave me time to think and get into the Word, which I definitely needed, and time to build my new relationship with Christ.

God started showing me things. At first, Scripture was confusing to me. I didn't understand it. The Bible seemed to contradict itself. I asked God, "Please show me something in here that's from you to me."

I asked him for wisdom and understanding and to open my eyes to his Word. As the effect of 20 years of drugs and alcohol left my body, I started understanding things in the Bible, and I began to notice my surroundings. I saw God at work, even in prison.

I asked God to let me be a light. Then the blessings began to happen. Guys started saying, "Man, I'm having problems. Can you pray for me?"

"Sure," I'd say. "Come over to my house." Our cells were our homes. A prisoner's home and his privacy are sacred and respected in prison. That's all a person has left.

I carried my Bible everywhere I went. More than once, I heard, "There goes a Bible thumper." I also heard, "Look at him. He's getting God while he's in prison. You watch him when he gets out."

I attended Bible studies and church groups in prison. There's no barrier between colors and races in those groups. We're all God's children. I caught a lot of slack for eating lunch with a black man or a Mexican. The bikers and the white supremacists would try to hassle me, try to break me, verbally and physically.

A couple times, I could have been in a physical confrontation, but the Lord gave me the words to say: "Hey, God loves you, man. He loves you, and I want to talk to you about him." And they'd be gone. They couldn't handle it.

"Thanks, Lord!" I'd say.

After I'd been in prison six or eight months, I was returned to Larimer County for reconsideration. When I walked into the courtroom, I prayed, "Lord, give me the words. Don't let me speak, but you speak through me." I sat quietly, listening to everything my public defender, who was trying to get my sentence reduced, had to say.

The district attorney was upset. "Oh, no," he insisted. "You can't reduce his sentence! This man needs to stay behind bars where he belongs."

After they finished arguing back and forth, the judge, who had seen me many times in his courtroom, looked at me. "Looks like you want to say something."

"Yes, Your Honor, I do."

"Get up. Let's hear it."

I told the judge the changes that had happened in my life. Then I said, "I'd really appreciate it if I could get the sentences to run concurrent, get them running together at the same time."

I had two, two-year sentences that ran consecutively, one after the other. The first one was for my habitual offender status and the second was for eluding. I thought it was kind of harsh, but I knew God had a plan.

The judge thought about it and said, "I can't do that, but I'll drop a year off your sentence."

I said, "Praise God!"

About a month later, I learned I was eligible for parole. My friends all warned me, "Nobody gets parole on their first time through."

"It's up to God," I told them. "If he wants me to stay, he's got a reason. If he wants me to go, praise him."

My mom and dad came down for my parole hearing, and we went before the parole board together. A single representative from the parole board sat across a desk from us.

I had all this stuff to show him—certificates of classes and seminars, things I'd done above and beyond what the system wanted me to do. I showed him all that and told him how my life was changing. He just looked at me then started ripping me to shreds.

"You do fine in prison," he said. "It's when you get out on the streets that you're a menace." He went on and on, and it got worse and worse. He even called me a murderer.

After pounding hard on me, he started in on my folks. "You did a lousy job raising your son," he told them. "As parents, you're failures!"

My mom started bawling. I wanted to reach over the desk and strangle the guy dead, but I couldn't. God had me pressed so hard in that seat I couldn't budge. I bit my tongue, thinking, *I can get through this. They're just trying to see how I react.*

Finally, I told the man, "I'm the one who did these things, and I'm the one paying the price. I'd appreciate it if you'd leave my parents out of it, because they had nothing to do with this. I made the bad choices in my life. I don't appreciate you making my mother cry."

My heart was pounding when I walked out of that meeting. *Well, Lord,* I thought, *it looks like I'm staying in prison. After that confrontation, there's no way I'm getting out of here.* I went outside and walked around the track several times to let off steam.

About a week later, however, I was told, "They accepted your parole."

"Praise God!" I exclaimed. "I guess I'm ready to go." But it took three or four months before I was released. About a month later, they sent me to a pre-release facility, where they provided classes to get inmates ready to re-integrate into society. When I got to pre-release, I called my old boss in Fort Collins, told him I was getting out soon, and asked if I could have my old job back.

He said, "Sure, come on back."

After I was released, I lived with my parents in Loveland and rode my bike to Fort Collins every day for work. After several weeks of commuting by bicycle, I said, "Lord, I know what you want me to do, but you've got to open doors for me. I need a place to live closer to work." I had looked all over for a place, and I was getting frustrated.

One day, as I walked outside after work to get on my bike, I looked across the street and saw a sign in front of some apartments that read, "Faith Property Management." It was like God was saying, "Have faith, wait on me." I called the number on the sign and moved in two days later.

Now I'm off parole, God has brought a wonderful Christian wife into my life, and he has provided me with a nice home and shop in Johnstown. People still ask me how I got my house with my bad credit. There's no way in the world's eyes I could have done it.

I tell them, "The glory goes to God. He gets the praise and glory for anything good in my life."

My daughters are 14 and 19. It's been a hard road for them because I was never a father to them. My oldest one gave her life to the Lord and is doing awesome. I'm just waiting on God for my youngest daughter. I have new kids in my new marriage. God says a happy man is a man with a full quiver of children. I've got a full quiver, and I'm happy.

I also have great Christian friends in Johnstown. I attend a Tuesday morning Bible study each week with several guys. The Lord is unlocking the doors of my understanding through that group.

I'm slowly but surely beginning to give back. I've been accepted to go into LCDC as a Freedom Fellowship volunteer, and I'll soon be allowed to go into the prisons. I love going to the jail because I am blessed so much. I get back a hundredfold more than I give. I'm anxious to get back into prison. I want to show those guys, "Hey, God loves all of us, and he doesn't want to see anybody go to hell."

Maybe I can influence some people others can't. I've got a record. I've got the tattoos. I've done it all. I'm here to say God was gracious enough to reach down and grab hold of me because he loves me and has a purpose for my life. He has a purpose for everybody. We just need to let him show us what it is.

Conclusion

Chaplain Donna Roth, Founder and Director

Looking back over my years of serving in the ministry God so unexpectedly called me to, I cannot imagine anything more rewarding. From our humble beginnings in Larimer County, Colorado, the Lord has literally taken us to the farthest reaches of the world to share his love with those who are incarcerated.

I thank all of you who faithfully support Freedom Fellowship. Because of you, we can go into the jails and prisons to "set the captives free." Without your help, there would be no Freedom Fellowship.

My prayer is that each reader will seek out the ministry God has for you, and that you will experience the incredible joy serving others brings. If God leads you to volunteer with Freedom Fellowship, expect incredible blessings in your life as God uses you to bring freedom to the captives. God bless you!

Chaplain Donna Roth
Founder and Director
Freedom Fellowship
Fort Collins, Colorado

To contact Freedom Fellowship:

info@freedom-fellowship.org / *www.freedom-fellowship.org*

970-310-5711

Freedom Fellowship
PO Box 726
Fort Collins, CO 80522

Becky Lyles is a freelance writer and editor. She lives with her husband in beautiful Boise, Idaho, and serves with her church's children's ministry. She also volunteers as a transitional coach for female ex-inmates seeking God-empowered lifestyle change. Learn about other books by Becky at *www.beckylyles.com.*

Contact Becky at: *beckylyles@beckylyles.com.*

www.ingramcontent.com/pod-product-compliance
Lightning Source LLC
LaVergne TN
LVHW051727080426
835511LV00018B/2928